THE
HOLY
EUCHARIST

THE HOLY EUCHARIST

St. Alphonsus Liguori

Edited and abridged by Msgr. Charles Dollen

ALBA·HOUSE house NEW·YORK

SOCIETY OF ST. PAUL, 2187 VICTORY BLVD., STATEN ISLAND, NEW YORK 10314

Library of Congress Cataloging-in-Publication Data

Liguori, Alfonso Maria de', Saint, 1696-1787
    [Selections, English. 1994]
    The Holy Eucharist / by St. Alphonsus Liguori; edited and
abridged by Charles Dollen.
    ISBN 0-8189-0676-6
    1. Lord's Supper — Catholic Church. 2. Mass. 3. Catholic Church —
Liturgy. 4. Catholic Church — Doctrines. I. Dollen, Charles.
II. Title.
BX2215.2,.L523213   1994
234'.163— dc20   93-5955
                                                  CIP

Produced and designed in the United States of America by the
Fathers and Brothers of the Society of St. Paul,
2187 Victory Boulevard, Staten Island, New York 10314,
as part of their communications apostolate.

ISBN: 0-8189-0676-6

Printing Information:

Current Printing - first digit	1	2	3	4	5	6	7	8	9	10

Year of Current Printing - first year shown

1994	1995	1996	1997	1998	1999

Dedicated

to the memory of

BISHOP CHARLES FRANCIS BUDDY

First Bishop of San Diego, CA

1936-1966

Table of Contents

Book Three:
Meditations for Corpus Christi

Book Four:
Novena to the Sacred Heart

Book Five:
The Practice of the Love of Jesus Christ

Book Six:
Novena to the Holy Spirit

Foreword

St. Alphonsus Liguori was born near Naples, Italy in 1696. He was Bishop of "St. Agatha of the Goths" and is noted for his foundation of the Congregation of the Most Holy Redeemer (the Redemptorists). His principal work was the *Theologiae Moralis* but he wrote extensively on prayer, the spiritual life, and on many of the controversies of his time. He died in 1787, was canonized in 1839, declared a Doctor of the Church in 1871 and named patron of confessors and moralists in 1950. His feast day is August 1.

This book is presented for the spiritual profit of priests who celebrate Mass and for the faithful who are present at it.

To the first part, "The Sacrifice of Jesus Christ," a number of other titles by Saint Alphonsus are included that are centered around various aspects of devotion to Christ or are suitable for use in devotions such as Holy Hours.

Since the time of Pope St. Pius X at the beginning of the 20th century, frequent, even daily Holy Communion has become the most salutary practice of our day. During the time of St. Alphonsus Liguori and St. Francis de Sales there was a much more rigorous approach which is reflected in this volume and in the *Introduction to the Devout Life*. There is no doubt whatsoever that both saints ardently longed for our current practice.

It is my hope that I have retained the doctrine and devotional aspect of Alphonsus Liguori's material with only a contemporary update in form and vocabulary. It is sincerely hoped that this has been done without the need of any apology to St. Alphonsus.

Book One

The Sacrifice of Jesus Christ

I.

Aspects of the Sacrifice of Jesus Christ

This little work is titled "The Sacrifice of Jesus Christ" for, although we distinguish by different names the "Sacrifice of the Cross" from the "Sacrifice of the Altar," yet it is substantially the same sacrifice. In fact we find at the altar the same victim and the same priest that one day offered himself on the cross. The Sacrifice of the Altar is a continuation or a renewal of the Sacrifice of the Cross and differs from it only in the manner in which it is offered.

A. THE SACRIFICES OF THE OLD LAW WERE FIGURES OF THE SACRIFICE OF JESUS CHRIST

All the sacrifices of the Old Law were figures of the sacrifice of our divine Redeemer, and there were four kinds of these sacrifices: the sacrifices of peace, of thanksgiving, of expiation and of petition.

1. The sacrifices of peace were instituted to render God the worship of adoration that is due to him as the sovereign master of all things. The holocausts are among them.
2. The sacrifices of thanksgiving were meant to give thanks to God for all his benefits.
3. The sacrifices of expiation were established to obtain pardon for sins. This kind of sacrifice was especially represented on the Day of Atonement (*Yom Kippur*) when the scapegoat was driven out into the desert, bearing the sins of all the people (Lv 16:8).

This sacrifice was the most expressive figure of the sacrifice of the cross. Jesus Christ was laden with all the sins of all mankind, as Isaiah had foretold: "The Lord placed on him the iniquity of all" (cf. Is 54:6). He was then led forth from Jerusalem, ignominiously, where the Apostle invites us to follow him by sharing in his burden: "Let us then go to him outside the camp, bearing the reproach he bore" (Heb 13:8). He was abandoned to ferocious beasts, that is, to the Gentiles who crucified him (cf. Heb 9:3-12).

> 4. Finally, the sacrifices of petition had for their object to obtain the help and grace of God.

Now, all of these sacrifices were abolished by the coming of the Redeemer, because only the sacrifice of Jesus Christ, which was the perfect sacrifice, was sufficient to expiate all sin and merit for mankind every grace. All the ancient sacrifices were imperfect and had to be repeated over and over again. This is why the Son of God, on entering the world, said to his Father: "Sacrifice and offering you did not desire, but a body you prepared for me; holocausts and sin offerings you took no delight in. Then I said, 'As is written of me in the scroll, Behold, I come to do your will, O God'" (Heb 10:5-7).

Therefore, by offering to God the sacrifice of Jesus Christ we can fulfill all our duties toward his supreme majesty and provide for all our wants. This way we succeed in maintaining a holy communication between God and ourselves.

The Old Law enumerated the five conditions regarding victims which were to be offered to God so as to be agreeable to him. They are sanctification, oblation, immolation, consumption and participation.

> 1. The victim had to be sanctified, or consecrated to God so that nothing unworthy or unholy would be offered to his majesty. The animal destined for sacrifice had to be without stain or defect. It could not be blind, lame, weak or deformed (Dt 15:21).

This condition indicated that such would be the Lamb of God, the victim promised for the salvation of the world, that he would be holy and free from every defect. Even our prayers and good works are not fully pleasing to God if they are defective.

The animal thus set apart for sacrifice could no longer be used for any profane or worldly use and was regarded as so consecrated that only a priest should touch it. This could indicate to us how displeasing it is to God if persons consecrated to him busy themselves with worldly things that are not truly necessary. They live distracted from what concerns the glory of God.

2. The victim had to be offered to God, often done with words prescribed by God.

3. It had to be immolated, that is, put to death. This was done, often by actually killing the sacrifice. However, other means of using up the material were prescribed as in the case of show-bread and other items.

4. The victim had to be consumed. If done by fire, it was a holocaust. This total destruction indicated the unlimited power God has over all his creatures and that as he created them out of nothing, so he can reduce them to the nothingness from which they came.

In fact, the principal end of the sacrifice is to acknowledge God as the sovereign being, so superior to all things that everything before him is purely nothing. All things are as nothing before him who possesses all things in himself.

5. Priests and people together were partakers of the victim. In the holocausts, the people partook of the victim by being present. In other sacrifices, the victim was divided into three parts; one for the priest, one for the people, and one for destruction.

These five conditions are found in the sacrifice of the Paschal Lamb (Ex 12:3).

B. FULFILLMENT OF THE PROPHETIC FIGURES

The Sacrifice of our Lord was a perfect sacrifice of which those sacrifices of the Old Law were but signs, figures and what the Apostle calls "weak and destitute elemental powers" (Gal 4:9). The sacrifice offered by Jesus Christ really fulfilled all the conditions mentioned above.

The first condition, sanctification, or the consecration of the victim, was accomplished in the Incarnation of the Word by God the Father himself, as St. John reports, "the one whom the Father has consecrated" (Jn 10:36). When the Archangel Gabriel announced to the Blessed Virgin that she was chosen to be the Mother of the Son of God, he said, "The child to be born will be called holy, the Son of God" (Lk 1:35).

This divine victim, who was to be sacrificed for the salvation of the world, had already been sanctified by God when he was born of Mary. From the first moment in which the Eternal Word took a human body, he was consecrated to God to be the victim of the great sacrifice that was to be accomplished on the Cross for the salvation of mankind. Therefore Christ said to the Father, "But a body you prepared for me . . . I come to do your will, O God" (Heb 10:5, 7).

The second condition, the oblation or offering, was also fulfilled at the moment of the Incarnation when Jesus Christ voluntarily offered himself to atone for the sins of mankind. Knowing that divine justice could not be satisfied by all the ancient sacrifices, nor by all the works of mankind, he offered himself to atone for all sins and said to God: "Sacrifice and offering you did not desire . . . holocausts and sin offerings you took no delight in. Then I said, 'Behold I come to do your will'" (Heb 10:5-7).

Then St. Paul adds immediately, "By this 'will' we have been consecrated through the offering of the body of Jesus Christ once for all" (Heb 10:10). This text is indeed remarkable. Sin had rendered mankind unworthy of being offered to God and of being accepted by him; therefore it was necessary that Jesus Christ should offer himself for us in order to sanctify us by his grace and to make us worthy of being accepted by God.

This offering which our Lord made then did not limit itself to that moment. It began then; it has continued since; it will continue forever. It will cease on earth only at the time of the Antichrist, as Daniel foretold (Dn 12:11).

The Sacrifice of Jesus Christ will never cease since the Son of God will always continue to offer himself to his Father by an eternal sacrifice, for he himself is the priest and the victim, not according to the order of Aaron of which the priesthood and the sacrifice were temporary, imperfect and inadequate to appease the anger of God against rebellious mankind, but according to the order of Melchizedek, as David predicted: "You are a priest forever according to the order of Melchizedek" (Ps 110:4).

The priesthood of Jesus Christ will be eternal, since even after the end of this world he will always continue to offer in heaven this same victim that he once offered on the Cross for the glory of God and for the salvation of mankind.

The third condition of sacrifice — the immolation of the victim — was obviously accomplished by the death of our Lord on the Cross.

Finally, we must look at the consumption and partaking which complete a perfect sacrifice. The consumption is accomplished by the Resurrection, when Christ shed all that was terrestrial and mortal and was clothed in divine glory. He had asked his Father to glorify him (Jn 17:5), but it was not the divine glory which he possessed from all eternity. It was for his humanity that he prayed.

The partaking in the perfect sacrifice was accomplished in Heaven where all the blessed are partakers of the victim's triumph.

The two conditions of consumption and communion are manifestly fulfilled in the Sacrifice of the Altar, which, as the Council of Trent declared, is the same as that of the Cross. In fact, the Sacrifice of the Mass instituted by our Lord before his death, is a continuation of the Sacrifice of the Cross.

Jesus Christ wished that the price of his blood, shed for the salvation of mankind, should be applied to us by the Sacrifice of the Altar. In it, the victim offered is the same, though present there in an unbloody manner. Thus the Council of Trent:

"Although Christ our Lord was to offer himself once to his Eternal Father on the altar of the Cross by actually dying to obtain for us eternal redemption, yet as his priesthood was not to become extinct by his death, in order to leave his Church a visible sacrifice suited to the present condition of mankind, a sacrifice which might at the same time re-present to us the bloody sacrifice consummated on the Cross, preserve the memory of it to the end of the world and apply the salutary fruits of it for the remission of the sin we daily commit . . .

"At his last supper, on the very night on which he was betrayed, giving proof that he was established a priest forever according to the order of Melchizedek, he offered to God the Father his body and blood, under the appearances of bread and wine, and, under the same symbols, gave them to the apostles, whom he constituted at the same time priests of the New Law.

"By these words, 'Do this in remembrance of me,' he commissioned them and their successors in the priesthood to consecrate and offer his body and blood, as the Catholic Church has always understood and taught" (Sess. 22, c.1).

In the very next chapter the Council declares that the Lord, appeased by the oblation of the Sacrifice of the Mass, grants us his graces and the remission of sins. "It is one and the same victim; the one that offers sacrifice is the same one who, after having sacrificed himself on the Cross, offers himself now by the ministry of the priest; there is no difference except in the manner of offering" (Sess. 22, c.2).

Jesus Christ has, then, paid the price of our redemption in the Sacrifice of the Cross. He wishes that the fruit of the ransom given should also be applied to us in the Sacrifice of the Altar, being himself the chief sacrificer who offers the same victim, namely his own body and his own blood — with this difference only, that on the Cross his blood was shed, while it is not shed at the altar.

The Roman Catechism teaches that the Sacrifice of the Mass does not serve only to praise God and to thank him for the gifts he has granted us, but it is a true propitiatory sacrifice by which we obtain from God pardon for our sins and the graces of which we stand in need. The fruit of the death of Jesus Christ is applied to us by the Sacrifice of the Altar.

In the Mass, we find not only the three essential parts of the Sacrifice of the Cross — the sanctification and offering of the victim but also the immolation which is here done mystically, the consecration of the body and that of the blood taking place separately. We also find the other two parts of sacrifice, namely the destruction or consumption by all who receive Holy Communion.

We see clearly how, in the Sacrifice of the Altar, the five conditions required for a perfect sacrifice make it the same as the Sacrifice of the Cross.

II.

Short Explanation of the Prayers of the Mass

(St. Alphonsus wrote about the Tridentine Mass, which differs in some particulars from the form of the Mass now generally celebrated. This should not detract from the value of what he says here. In this abridgment, some of the shorter prayers found in the Mass have not been covered.)

(In the name of the Father, and of the Son, and of the Holy Spirit. Amen.) Since only God has power over the life of his Incarnate Son, who is the victim of the Sacrifice of the Mass, the priest needs divine authority in order to be able to offer Jesus Christ to his heavenly Father in this sacrifice. He has this through Holy Orders and, hence, is able to say, in union with Jesus Christ who is the principal one who offers the sacrifice, "In the name of the Father, and of the Son, and of the Holy Spirit"; thus declaring that he offers the sacrifice by the authority of the three Persons of the Blessed Trinity.

(We beseech You, O Lord, by the merits of Your saints, etc.)

Having reached the altar, he kisses it, to unite himself to Jesus Christ, represented by the altar; and, through the merits of the holy martyrs whose relics are therein enclosed, he asks our Lord to deign to pardon him all his sins.

From the first ages the Church was accustomed to offer up the Eucharistic sacrifice on the tombs of the martyrs who had sacrificed their lives for God, and who for this reason have always been particularly honored in the Church. During the first period of the Church there were no other festivals than those of the mysteries of Jesus Christ, those of the Blessed Virgin, and the anniversaries of the martyrs. However, it is not to the saints, but only to God that altars are erected. As St. Augustine says, "We have not erected an altar to the martyr, Stephen, but with the relics of the martyr Stephen we have erected an altar to God" (Sermon 318).

It is usually in the Introit that the Church proposes the subject of the feast that is celebrated. Mention is therein made of some divine mystery, of the Blessed Virgin, or of some other saint whom the Church honors on that day, so that we simply render this honor to the saint, since the sacrifice is offered only to God.

(*Kyrie, eleison; Christe, eleison.*) These are Greek words that mean, "Lord, have mercy; Christ, have mercy." Pope Sylvester ordered that, after the example of the Greeks the *Kyrie eleison* should be said in the Latin Church. Thereby is shown the union that exists between the Greek and the Latin Church.

(*Glory to God in the highest*, etc.) This canticle or prayer is formed of the words that the celestial choirs used when the Angel came to announce to the shepherds the birth of the Savior: "Glory to God in the highest, and peace to his people on earth" (Lk 2:14). The remaining words were added by the Church. In it God is thanked for his glory, because God has used our salvation for his glory by saving us through Jesus Christ. In offering himself as a sacrifice to his Father, Jesus Christ has procured salvation for men, and has given, at the same time, infinite glory to God. Then the Church, addressing herself to Jesus Christ, asks him by the merits of his sacrifice to have pity on us; and she concludes by proclaiming: "For you alone are the Holy

One; You alone are the Lord; You alone are the Most High, Jesus Christ, with the Holy Spirit, in the glory of God the Father. Amen." For our Savior, who sacrifices himself as a victim, is at the same time God, equal to him to whom the sacrifice is offered.

Then follows the Prayer or Collect, thus called because the priest, performing the office of mediator between God and men, collects all the prayers of the people, and presents them to God. The Collect is said in a suppliant manner, with outstretched and raised hands. In these prayer are asked of God the graces that have reference to the mystery of the day: for example, at Easter, the grace to rise with Jesus Christ, and at the Ascension to dwell with him in spirit in heaven; or we ask for those graces that we wish to obtain through the intercession of the saint whose feast we are celebrating. But all these prayers are concluded with "through our Lord Jesus Christ" because all the graces that we obtain are given to us chiefly in view of his merits.

It is not true, as the innovators say, that we offer the Sacrifice of the Altar to the saints. We know very well that the sacrifice can be offered only to God. If at the Mass we make mention of the saints, we do so only because of the favors that they have received from God, to whom they acknowledge they are indebted for all the happiness that they possess.

Here follow the Epistle and the Gospel.

While listening to the reading of the Epistle, we must hear it as if it were God himself who speaks by the mouth of his prophets and apostles.

We should listen to the Gospel as if we were hearing the words of our divine Savior instructing us himself, and we should at the same time ask him for the necessary help to put into practice what he teaches. It is an ancient custom to stand during the reading of the Gospel, to show that we are ready to follow the precepts and counsels that our Lord points out to us. While the priest is reciting the Creed, we should renew our faith in all the mysteries and all the dogmas that the Church teaches.

In offering the bread and wine the priest calls them *the immaculate Host, the Chalice of salvation.* We should not be astonished at this; for all the prayers and all the ceremonies before and after the consecration have reference to the divine Victim. It is at the moment of consecration that the Victim presents himself to God, that he offers himself to him, and that the sacrifice is offered; but as these different acts cannot be explained at the same time, they are explained one after the other.

The priest then offers by anticipation the bread prepared for the sacrifice while saying, "Accept, O holy Father, this immaculate Host, etc.," and he offers the wine as if it had already been consecrated by saying, "We offer unto You, O Lord, the Chalice of salvation, etc.," because this wine, being afterwards changed into the blood of Jesus Christ, becomes our salvation.

St. Augustine says that as at the Eucharistic Table our Savior offers us to eat and to drink his body and his blood, we should also offer to him our body and our blood by giving ourselves entirely to him, being ready to sacrifice our life for his glory, should that be necessary. These are the beautiful words of the holy Doctor: "You know what this banquet is, and what nourishment is offered you at this table. Since Jesus Christ gives entirely his body and his blood, let no one approach without giving himself entirely to the Lord" (*Tract on John*, 47).

A little water is mixed with the wine to represent the mixture or union that takes place in the Incarnation of the Word between the divinity and the humanity, and also to represent the intimate union that is effected in the sacramental Communion between Jesus Christ and the person who communicates. St. Augustine calls this union "a mixture of God and of man." Hence the priest, in the prayer which he recites while mixing the water with the wine, beseeches God to grant that, as his divine Son became partaker of our humanity, we may be made partakers of his divinity.

The Council of Trent declares that this mingling of water and wine in the chalice is prescribed: "The holy Synod admonishes that it is enjoined on the priests by the Church that they should mix water with the wine that is to be offered in the chalice, as it is believed that the Lord has done the same thing" (Sess. 22, c.7). However, this is only an ecclesiastical, not a divine precept. The chalice of salvation is offered to the Lord, so that it may arise in his divine presence as an agreeable odor, for our salvation and for the salvation of the whole world.

The priest presents himself before our Lord with a humble and contrite heart, and begs him to bless the great sacrifice that is about to be offered. Then he goes to wash his hands, out of respect for this divine sacrifice.

(*Receive, O Holy Trinity,* etc.) By this prayer the priest offers to God Jesus Christ as a victim already immolated by his death on the Cross. Heretics calumniate us when they affirm that we offer to God two different sacrifices, namely, the sacrifice of the Cross and that of the Altar. We reply to them that there are not two sacrifices, since the sacrifice of the Altar is a memorial of the sacrifice of the Cross. It is really the same sacrifice as that of the Cross, Jesus Christ being there the principal offerer and the victim that is offered.

(*Pray, brethren that our sacrifice,* etc.) By these words, the priest exhorts the people to supplicate the Lord to receive this sacrifice for the glory of his name and the good of the faithful. The server then answers in the name of the people by praying to God to accept this sacrifice.

Then follows the *Secret,* a silent prayer that refers to the offerings made by the people, namely of the bread and wine that are to be changed into the body and blood of Jesus Christ. The Church asks the Lord to bless them and to render them profitable, not only to those who present them, but to all the faithful.

The priest then exhorts the faithful to raise their hearts to God: "Lift up your hearts." The people answer that they have already done so: "We have lifted them up to the Lord." And the priest continues by inviting them to unite with him in thanking the Lord: "Let us give thanks to the Lord, our God."

The celebrant entreats the Lord to accept our prayers united with those of the angels who celebrate his glory by repeating without ceasing the canticle, "Holy, Holy, Holy, Lord God of Hosts!" (Is 6:3). He concludes by repeating the words used by the Jewish people in their acclamations at the triumphant entry of Jesus into Jerusalem:

"Blessed is he who comes in the name of the Lord, Hosanna in the highest!" (Mt 21:9).

Then begins what we call the Canon of the Mass, which the Council of Trent (Sess. 22, c.4) declares to be free from every error, since it is composed of the very words of our Lord, of the traditions of the apostles, and of the pious regulations of the Holy See. The priest first prays to his heavenly Father, in the name of the whole Church and through the merits of Jesus Christ, to accept and to bless the offerings that are made to him.

The Holy Sacrifice is, before all, offered for the Catholic Church by praying to God that he may preserve her in peace, defend her, maintain her in unity, and govern her through the ministry of the pastors, by communicating to them his Holy Spirit.

The priest recommends, at first, all those persons for whom he wishes most especially to pray; then he recommends all those who, happening to be present, offer with him the Holy Sacrifice; finally, he recommends all their relatives and friends.

It must be observed that there is a great difference between sacrificing and offering: to the priest alone belongs the right to sacrifice, whereas all those who are present may offer the sacrifice. In order to participate in the fruit of the sacrifice we must have faith and devotion, which spring from charity. The first effect of the sacrifice of the Cross, which is applied to us by the sacrifice of the Altar, is to become free from the power of the devil. God grants to us spiritual and temporal graces by virtue of this sacrifice, through which alone we can render to God the thanks that we owe him.

(*In union with the whole Church we honor Mary*, etc.) This prayer is said in order to enter into communion with the Church Triumphant. Thereby we honor, in the first place, the memory of the Mother of God, then that of the apostles, then that of the martyrs and of all the other saints, through the merits and the intercession of whom we beg bur Lord's protection in all our necessities. We who are travellers upon earth form only one body with the saints who are in Heaven, and united with them in the same spirit, we offer to God the same sacrifice.

(*Father, accept this offering from your whole family*, etc.)

The priest spreads his hands over the bread and the wine, and, through the merits of Jesus Christ, who redeemed us from the power of the devil, he prays to the Eternal Father favorably to accept this offering that his servants and his whole family make to him. He also asks God to help us to enjoy peace in this life, to preserve us from hell, and to admit us among the number of the elect.

(*Bless and approve our offering: make it acceptable to you, an offering in spirit and in truth. Let it become for us the body and blood of Jesus Christ, your only Son, our Lord.*) In this prayer the priest asks God to cause this oblation to be blessed, that by this blessing the bread and the wine may be changed into the body and the blood of Jesus Christ; that it may be consecrated to the divine Majesty and approved as a perfect sacrifice.

(*The day before he suffered*, etc.) Here the priest, renewing the memory of the Passion of Jesus Christ, relates what the Lord did on the evening before his death, when he instituted the Sacrament and the sacrifice of his body and blood. Then the priest does the same thing, and consecrates the bread and wine by pronouncing the very words used by Jesus Christ.

The form of the consecration is taken from Matthew 26:26: "This is my body." These words need no explanation, since they themselves declare what mystery is accomplished, namely, the change of the bread into the body of Jesus Christ.

The form of the consecration of the chalice is as follows: "This is the cup of my blood, the blood of the new and everlasting covenant. It will be shed for you, and for all, so that sins may be forgiven." These words the Church has taken partly from St. Luke and partly from St. Matthew.

This divine mystery is called the *Mystery of Faith*, not to exclude the reality of the blood of Jesus Christ, but to show that in it the faith shines forth in a wonderful manner, and triumphs over all the difficulties that may be raised by human reason, since it is here, says Innocent III, that we see one thing and believe another.

(*Do this in memory of me.*) After the two consecrations the priest repeats the words of Jesus Christ, by which our Savior commanded his apostles and their successors to do, in memory of his Passion, what he had just done himself in their presence.

The priest then calls to mind the Passion of our Lord, his resurrection, and ascension. He offers to the divine Majesty in the name of the Church the consecrated victim, which he calls "the bread of life, and the cup of eternal salvation." While pronouncing these words he blesses the bread and the chalice with the sign of the cross.

Then the priest prays to the Lord that he may accept with pleasure this sacrifice, just as he accepted the offerings of Abel, the sacrifice of Abraham, and that of Melchizedek. In recalling to mind these three sacrifices, we regard less the value of the things offered than the sanctity of those who offered them, because they were holy men. Consequently, if God, because of his sanctity, favorably received their sacrifice, how much more should please him the sacrifice of the Saint of saints — of our Lord Jesus Christ!

The priest continues humbly to ask the Savior that the consecrated Host be presented to his divine Majesty through the hands of his holy Angel, in order that all those who are going to receive the body and the blood of his adorable Son may be filled with blessings and all celestial gifts through the merits of Jesus Christ.

The priest asks the Lord to remember his servants who have passed to the other life and to grant them a place of refreshment, light, and peace, through the merits of Jesus Christ. When the charity of the souls that depart from this life is not sufficient to purify them, the fire of purgatory will supply this defect. Yet the charity of the Savior supplies it best by means of the Eucharistic sacrifice, which procures for these holy souls great mitigation of their sufferings, and often deliverance from their torments. The Council of Trent (Sess. 25, *Decree on Purgatory*) says: "The souls there detained are helped by the suffrages of the faithful, but principally by the acceptable sacrifice of the altar." And it adds (Sess. 22, c.2) that this is a tradition of the apostles. St. Augustine exhorts us to offer the sacrifice for all the dead, in case the souls that we recommend cannot receive our help.

(*Have mercy on us all.*) Here the Church prays for sinners, in order that God may vouchsafe, in his mercy, to permit them to enter the society of the saints; and she asks this grace through the merits of Jesus Christ.

The Church Militant regards herself as entirely composed of sinners. She thinks herself unworthy to call God her "Father" which in the name of the faithful she will now do as she addresses the seven petitions of the Lord's Prayer to God. Hence she protests that she only dares to address this prayer to God because God himself has commanded her to do so. Regarding our poverty and our insufficiency, Jesus Christ himself deigned to compose our prayer and to indicate the subjects on which we should address Almighty God. He instructs us to say:

"Our Father who art in heaven." The Apostle St. John says, "See what love the Father has bestowed on us that we may be called the children of God. Yet so we are" (1 Jn 3:1).

It is only because of divine love that we lowly creatures are able to become children of God, not by nature but by the grace of adoption. Such is the immense grace that the Son of God has obtained for us by becoming man.

St. Paul tells us: "You have received the spirit of adoption of sons, whereby we cry Abba, Father" (Rm 8:15). Can a subject wish for greater happiness than to be adopted by his king, or a creature to be adopted by its Creator? This is what God has done for us and he wishes that we should address him with filial confidence in this prayer.

"Hallowed be thy name." God cannot possess a greater sanctity than that which he possesses from all eternity, because he is infinite. Therefore, what we ask for in this petition is merely that God may make himself and his holy name known in every place, that he may make himself loved by everyone — by unbelievers who do not know him, by heretics who do not know him properly, and by sinners who know him but do not love him.

"Thy kingdom come." God exercises two kinds of dominion over our souls —the dominion of grace and the dominion of glory. By these words we ask for both, namely that the grace of God may reign among us in this life, that it may direct and govern us, so that one day

we may be judged worthy of glory and may have the happiness to possess God and be possessed by him for all eternity.

"Thy will be done on earth as it is in heaven." The whole perfection of a soul consists in the perfect accomplishment of the will of God as is done by the blessed in Heaven. Therefore Jesus Christ wishes us to ask the grace to accomplish the will of God on earth as the angels and saints accomplish it in Heaven.

"Give us this day our daily bread." This is the reading in St. Luke (11:3). By this prayer we ask God for the temporal goods of which we stand in need to sustain our present life. The words "our daily bread" teach us that we should ask for this kind of goods with moderation, after the example of Solomon who asked for only what is necessary: "Provide me with the food of life" (Pr 30:8).

The reading from St. Matthew (6:11) says: "Give us this day our supersubstantial bread." By this we must understand Jesus Christ himself in the Sacrament of the Altar, that is in Holy Communion. We ask for this heavenly bread every day because every good Christian should communicate every day, if not really, then spiritually, at least.

"And forgive us our trespasses as we forgive those who trespass against us." To eat worthily of this heavenly bread we must be free from mortal sin, or at least be washed from it by the blood of the Lamb in the sacrament of penance. One should also be free from an actual affection for some venial sin to receive communion with greater effects.

"And lead us not into temptation." How should we understand this petition? God does not lead us into temptation, as St. James reminds us. "God is not subject to temptation to evil and he himself tempts no one" (Jm 1:13). We must understand this phrase as we do the phrase from Isaiah, "Blind the heart of this people . . . lest they see" (Is 6:10). God never blinds any sinner, but he often refuses to grant to some, in punishment for their ingratitude, the light he would have given had they remained faithful and grateful.

This is the sense of "lead us not into temptation": we ask God not to permit us to have the misfortune of being in those occasions of sin in which we might fall. Therefore we should always watch and pray as the Lord exhorts us to do in order not to fall into temptation: "Watch and pray that you do not fall into temptation" (Mt 26:41). To enter into temptation means the same as to find one's self in the danger of falling into sin.

"But deliver us from evil." There are three kinds of evil from which we should ask the Lord to deliver us — the temporal evils of the body, the spiritual evils of the soul, and the eternal evils of the next life.

The temporal evils of this life we should be able to receive with resignation if God sends them for the good of our souls, such as, at times, poverty, sickness or desolation. When we ask God to deliver us from these, we should always do so on the condition that they are not necessary nor useful to our salvation.

The true evils from which we should absolutely pray to be delivered are spiritual evils which cause eternal evils. Moreover let us be convinced of this certainty, that in the present state of fallen human nature we cannot be saved unless we pass through the many tribulations with which this life is filled. In this life "it is necessary for us to undergo many hardships to enter the kingdom of God" (Ac 14:22).

Immediately after the Our Father the priest asks the Lord for himself and for all the faithful to grant, through the intercession of the Blessed Virgin, of the apostles and of all the saints, a continual peace during the days of the present life, so that his divine mercy may preserve them from every sin and from all confusion.

He then says, *"May the peace of the Lord be with you always."* He wishes the peace of the Lord for all his brethren, who answer him with the same wish: *"And also with you."*

He makes at the same time upon the chalice, with the particle of the Host which he holds in his hand, three signs of the cross, and then drops the sacred particle into the chalice and says, "May this mingling of the body and blood of our Lord Jesus Christ bring eternal life to us who receive it." This mixture of the holy species represents the union of the divinity with the humanity which was at first effected in the womb of Mary through the Incarnation of the Word, and which is renewed in the souls of the faithful when they receive him in the Eucharistic Communion.

"Lamb of God, you take away the sins of the world." Before Communion the Lamb of God, Jesus Christ, as the victim of the sacrifice, is invoked three times, to point out the need that we have of his grace, in order to be reconciled with God and to receive his peace.

Here follow the three prayers that precede Communion.

In the first prayer — *"Lord Jesus Christ, who said to your apostles, I leave you peace"* — prayer is offered to God that he may vouchsafe to grant peace to the Church in consideration of her faith, and keep her in union, according to his will, by delivering her from the division produced by false doctrines, and from all that is contrary to the divine will. And here the Church has introduced the custom that the faithful should give one another the kiss of peace, to remind them that their hearts should be united in charity. Before giving the kiss of peace, the priest kisses the altar to show that he cannot give the peace unless he has first received it from Jesus Christ, who is represented by the altar.

In the second prayer. *"Lord Jesus Christ, Son of the living God,"* the priest asks Jesus Christ, by virtue of his adorable body and blood, to deliver him from all evils, and to keep him always united with him.

In the third prayer he beseeches the Lord that this Communion may not turn to his condemnation, but may be for the salvation of his soul and body. The Holy Eucharist protects the soul against temptations and passions; it extinguishes the fire of concupiscence that burns in our bodies, and is a powerful remedy against the death of the soul.

"May the Body (Blood) of our Lord Jesus Christ preserve my soul to life everlasting." While pronouncing these words the priest receives the body and the blood of Jesus Christ. This prayer recalls to our mind that this precious body and blood are given to us as a pledge to eternal life, and as a viaticum in order to pass from this exile to our heavenly country. Hence when we receive Communion we ought to be so disposed as if we had to leave the earth at once, to enter eternity.

After having taken the precious blood the priest renews his thanks to God in the following words: *"Grant, O Lord, that what we have taken with our mouth we may receive with a pure heart, that though a temporal gift it may become for us an eternal remedy."* By this prayer the Church makes us ask God that, as our mouth has received this divine food and drink, our hearts may also receive them, so that they may be for us an eternal remedy that may forever heal us of all our infirmities.

Finally the priest says. *"May your body, O Lord, which I have received, and the blood which I have drunk, remain with me forever."* In this prayer, and in the last prayer called Post-Communion, he asks, through the merits of Jesus Christ in this mystery, and through the intercession of the saints whose memory is celebrated, that this divine Savior may always preserve him in this intimate union with him, and that no stain may rest on his soul, which has been nourished by a sacrament so holy and so pure.

"Go, the Mass is ended"; or, *"Let us bless the Lord."* It is with these words that the priest dismisses the people, and those who are present say, *"Thanks be to God."* "To give thanks to God," says St. Augustine, "is to acknowledge that all good things come from God, and to thank him for them."

This explanation of the prayers of the Mass may be serviceable to all — to the faithful as well as to priests.

III.

On Hearing Mass

In order to hear Mass with devotion, it is necessary to know that the Sacrifice of the Altar is the same as that once offered on Calvary with this difference, that on Calvary the blood of Jesus Christ was really shed but on the altar it is shed only in a mystical, unbloody, manner.

Had you been present on Calvary, with what devotion and tenderness you would have attended that great sacrifice! Enliven your faith, then, and consider that the same action is performed on the altar and that the same sacrifice is offered not only by the priest but also by all who attend Mass. Thus, all perform, in a certain manner, the office of priests during the celebration of the Mass, in which the merits of the Passion of our Savior are applied to us in a particular manner.

It is also necessary to understand that the Sacrifice of the Mass has been instituted for four ends:

1. to honor God (*adoration*);
2. to satisfy for our sins (*contrition*);
3. to thank God for his benefits (*thanksgiving*);
4. to obtain divine graces (*supplication*).

This leads to the following considerations which may be of help to us in hearing Mass with great fruit:

1. By the oblation — the offering of the person of Jesus Christ, God and man, to the Eternal Father — we give to God infinite honor; we give him greater honor than he would receive from the oblation of the lives of every man and woman, and of all the angels combined.
2. By the oblation of Jesus Christ in the Mass we offer to God a complete satisfaction for all the sins of mankind and especially for the sins of those who are present and participating in the Mass; to whom is applied the divine blood by which the human race was redeemed on Calvary.

Thus by each Mass more satisfaction is made to God than by any other expiatory work. Although the Mass is of infinite value, God accepts it only in a finite manner, according to the dispositions of those who attend the holy sacrifice. Therefore it is useful to hear several Masses.

3. In the Mass we give to God an adequate thanksgiving for all the benefits he has bestowed on us.
4. During the Mass we can obtain all the graces that we desire for ourselves and others. We are unworthy to receive any grace from God, but Jesus Christ has given us the means of obtaining all graces if, while we offer him to God in the Mass, we ask them of the Eternal Father in his name, for then Jesus himself unites with us in prayer.

If you knew that while you pray to the Lord, the Blessed Mother, along with the whole of Paradise, united with you, with what confidence would you pray? Now when you ask of God any grace during the Mass, Jesus, whose prayers are more efficacious than the prayers of all who are in Heaven, prays for you and offers in your behalf the merits of his Passion.

IV.

On Making a Good Confession

Preparation: To prepare ourselves well for confession, we should retire from every external source of distraction, go to a church or chapel, place ourselves in the presence of God, and make an act of adoration to the Holy Trinity.

Examination of Conscience: We ought to represent confession to ourselves as the last one of our lives and dispose ourselves to make it as one would do who is at the point of death. We should ask God for the grace to make well the examination of conscience, and for the necessary light and wisdom to know well our sins. Offer a prayer to the Holy Spirit.

For those who approach the sacraments often, the examination should be brief and unaccompanied by fear, disquiet, or scrupulosity.

A momentary view of the faults that hold us back from God should be sufficient. Anything of a grave nature will stand out immediately, so the rest of the preparation time is best spent in encouraging the dispositions of contrition and devotion.

As for those who seldom approach the sacraments, it is necessary to spend enough time for a diligent examination of their consciences. They may want to read over the commandments of God and the Church, the seven capital sins, the duties of their state in life and so forth. If the exact number of each or any grave sin cannot be remembered, an approximation is sufficient. God does not oblige us to do what is morally impossible.

Motives for Contrition: Reflect that sin, however trifling it may be, really offends Almighty God and insults the infinite perfection of him whose greatness knows no limits and who is, consequently, deserving of infinite love. By sin you displease one who loves you most tenderly. Reflect on this and you will see how foolish sin really is. We will never understand, in this life, the malice of sin or the punishment it deserves.

Reflect that God is our sovereign benefactor who has freely given us innumerable benefits, both general and particular. He has drawn us out of nothing and formed us in his own image and likeness without having any need for us at all. He has redeemed us with the precious blood of his Son and made us Christians. He has been so patient with us and given us ways and means to save our souls. Will we repay his many mercies with ingratitude?

Reflect that the Most Blessed Trinity, Father, Son and Holy Spirit, the only and almighty God, is present everywhere, that he sees all things, knows all things, and penetrates the inmost secrets of our hearts. All the choirs of angels are in adoration before him, yet we have the audacity to sin in his presence! Reflect also that this God before whom we sin is also our sovereign Judge who will pass sentence on us at the hour of death. Then, make an act of contrition.

V.

On Receiving Holy Communion

Preparation: St. Francis de Sales says in his *Introduction to the Devout Life* (2:21) that our Savior can never be seen more amiable and more tender, in all that he has done for us, than in Holy Communion where he gives himself as our food that he may unite himself to the hearts and bodies of all his faithful. There is no means more efficacious than Holy Communion to enkindle devotion and the holy love of God in our souls.

If we speak of doing something agreeable to God, what can a soul do more agreeable to him than to receive Communion? Dionysius the Areopagite teaches us that love always tends towards perfect union, but how can a soul be more perfectly united with Jesus than in the manner of which he speaks himself, saying, "He who eats my flesh and drinks my blood abides in me and I in him" (Jn 6:57). St. Augustine adds that if you receive Communion every day, Jesus will always be with you and you will always advance in divine love.

Again, if there is a question of healing our spiritual infirmities, what more certain remedy can we have than the Holy Communion which is called by the Council of Trent, "a remedy whereby we may be freed from daily faults and be preserved from mortal sins" (Sess. 13, c.2).

Why is it, then, that in so many souls we see so little fruit with frequent Communion and the constant relapse into the same faults? The fault is not in the food but in the disposition of the one who receives.

Solomon asks, "Can a man hide fire in his bosom and his garments not burn?" (Pr 6:27). "God is a consuming fire" (Dt 4:24). He comes himself in Holy Communion to enkindle this divine fire. How is it then that we can see such a strange phenomenon — souls remaining cold in divine love in the midst of such flames?

This failure to reap more abundant fruit comes from the want of perfect dispositions and especially from want of fervent preparation. Fire immediately inflames dry not green wood, for this latter is not disposed to burn. The saints derived great fruit from their Communions because they prepared themselves with very great care. St. Aloysius Gonzaga devoted three days to his preparation for Holy Communion and three days in thanksgiving to his Lord.

To prepare better for Holy Communion, a soul should be disposed on two main points: it should be detached from creatures, and it should have a great desire to advance in divine love.

1. First, a soul should detach itself from all things and drive everything from its heart which is not God. "Whoever has bathed," says the Lord, "has no need except to have his feet washed" (Jn 13:10). This signifies, as St. Bernard explains, that in order to receive this sacrament with great fruit we should not only be cleansed from mortal sins, but our feet should also be washed, that is, freed from earthly affections.

St. Gertrude asked our Lord what preparation he required of her for Holy Communion and he replied, "I only ask that you come to me empty of yourself to receive me."

2. It is most meritorious in Holy Communion to have a great desire to receive Jesus Christ and his holy love. In this sacred banquet only those who are famishing receive their fill. The blessed Virgin Mary had already said this: "He has filled the hungry with good things" (Lk 1:53) .

John of Avila wrote that as Jesus came into this world only after centuries of longing for him, so he enters a soul more fully that is longing for him. To profit most fully, St. Francis de Sales says that our principal object should be to advance in the love of God.

There is no prayer more agreeable to God or more profitable to the soul than that which is made during the thanksgiving after

Communion. Many theologians teach that Holy Communion, as long as the sacramental species lasts, constantly produces greater and greater graces in the soul, provided the soul is then constant in disposing itself by new acts of virtue.

Pope Eugenius IV taught that the Blessed Sacrament produces the same effect in the soul as material food in the body, which, when it enters the body, takes effect according to the state in which it finds itself. No wonder then that holy souls endeavor to remain as long as possible in prayer after Communion!

After Holy Communion, it is good to spend some time in very personal prayer using acts of love, affection, gratitude and the like. It is also a very powerful time for petitions. Prayers offered right after Holy Communion are more precious and profitable than prayers offered at any other time. The soul, being united with Jesus, has the value of its acts increased by the presence of Jesus. St. Teresa of Avila says that after Holy Communion, Jesus places himself in the soul as on a throne of grace and says, "What would you have me do for you?"

It is wise to prolong your time spent in thanksgiving after Communion, and during the whole day try to keep yourself united to Jesus by prayers and affections.

Book Two

Visits to the Blessed Sacrament
and the Blessed Virgin

I.

Visits to the Most Blessed Sacrament

(This was St. Alphonsus's first published writing. Since that date in 1745 it has been one of the most published of his treatises. This was presented as a contemporary prayerbook. Therefore we will give only the introductory material.)

Our holy faith teaches us, and we are bound to believe, that in the consecrated host Jesus Christ is really present under the species of bread. But we must also understand that he is thus present on our altars as on a throne of love and mercy, to dispense graces and there to show us the love which he bears for us by being pleased to dwell night and day hidden in our midst.

It is well known that Holy Church instituted the festival of Corpus Christi to be celebrated solemnly so that Christians would be moved to acknowledge and honor gratefully this loving presence and dwelling of Jesus Christ in the Sacrament of the Altar.

Yet how many have turned aside from this wonderful gift! Our Lord mentioned this to St. Margaret Mary Alacoque one time when she knelt in prayer before the Most Holy Sacrament. He showed her his heart on a throne of flames, crowned with thorns and surmounted by a cross. He said to her:

"Behold this heart which has loved men and women so much and which has spared itself nothing; and has even gone so far as to consume itself to show its love. But in return the greater part of the people only show me ingratitude and this by the irreverence, tepidity, sacrileges, and contempt which they offer me in this sacrament of love."

Jesus then asked for a special feast to be established in honor of his adorable Sacred Heart. He asked that on that day, all souls who love him should try, by their homage and the affection of their souls, to make amends for the insults which have been offered him in this Sacrament of the Altar. At the same time he promised abundant graces to all who would honor him in this way.

We can understand what our Lord said of old that his delight was to be with the children of mankind (Pr 8:31) and even when they abandon him or despise him, he is faithful to his love for all. How agreeable then, are those souls who visit him frequently and remain in his presence in the churches where he is present under the sacramental species.

Those devout souls who often go to spend their time with the Most Blessed Sacrament testify to the gifts and inspirations they have received, the flames of love which are there enkindled in their souls, and the joy they feel in the presence of this hidden God.

St. Aloysius Gonzaga was so attracted to the Blessed Sacrament that he had to be forbidden, under obedience, from spending too much time there when his other duties called. St. Mary Magdalene de Pazzi was told by our Lord to visit him frequently and she always went up as close to the altar as possible.

St. Francis Xavier, that seemingly indefatigable missionary, said that he refreshed himself and drew strength for his labors from his nightly visits to the Blessed Sacrament. He spent his days toiling for souls and his nights in prayer. St. John Francis Regis had the same devotion, and if the Church was closed for the night when he arrived, he would kneel outside despite cold or rain to make his visit.

St. Francis of Assisi used to go to communicate all his labors and undertakings to Jesus in the Most Holy Sacrament. So deep was the devotion of St. Wenceslaus, the Duke of Bohemia, that he sought out the finest wheat and the best grapes which he then prepared for the bread and wine for the Mass.

All the saints were enamored of this devotion, visiting the Most Blessed Sacrament, since it is impossible to find on earth a more precious gem or a treasure more worthy of our love, than Jesus in the Most Holy Sacrament. Certainly among all devotions, after that of receiving the sacraments, that of adoring Jesus in the Blessed Sacrament holds the first place, is the most pleasing to God, and most useful to ourselves.

Do not then, O devout soul, refuse to begin this devotion. Forsaking the conversation of men and women, dwell each day, from this time forward, for at least a half or a quarter of an hour in some church in the presence of Jesus Christ under the sacramental species. "O taste and see that the Lord is good" (Ps 34:9).

Try this devotion and by experience you will see the great benefit that you will derive from it. Be assured that the time you will spend with this devotion before the Most Divine Sacrament will be the most profitable to you in life and the source of your greatest consolation in death and in eternity.

Be aware that in a quarter hour's prayer spent in the presence of the Blessed Sacrament you will perhaps gain more than in all the other spiritual exercises of the day. It is true that in every place God graciously hears the petitions of those who pray to him, having promised to do so. "Ask and you shall receive" (Jn 16:24). However, have no doubt that Jesus dispenses his graces in greater abundance to those who visit him in the Most Holy Sacrament.

I feel bound to declare that it was through this practice, though tepidly followed in my first twenty-six years, that I found my vocation and turned my back on the world to turn myself completely to God. All else is folly in the light of eternity — festivals, theaters, parties and amusements. These are the "goods" of the world but how quickly passing they are and how often even the memory is bitter.

Be assured that Jesus Christ finds means to console a soul that remains with a recollected spirit before the Most Blessed Sacrament, far beyond what the world can do with its feasts and pastimes. What a joy it is to remain with faith and devotion before an altar and converse familiarly with Jesus Christ who is there for the express purpose of listening to and generously hearing those who pray to him.

Pray to ask his pardon for the displeasures which we have caused him; to represent our wants and needs to him, as a friend does to a friend in whom he places all his confidence; to ask him for his graces, for his love and for his kingdom; but above all, what a heaven it is there to remain making acts of love towards that Lord who is in the very tabernacle praying to the Eternal Father for us and is there burning with love for us.

Indeed, it is that love which keeps him there, hidden and unknown, and even when he is ignored by ungrateful souls! But why should we say more? "Taste and see."

II.

Visits to the Blessed Virgin

Now as to visits to the Most Blessed Virgin, the opinion of St. Bernard is well known and generally believed: that God dispenses no graces otherwise than through the hands of Mary. In his words: "God wills that we should receive nothing that does not pass through Mary's hands" (*Sermon on the Vigil of the Nativity*, #3).

It is the sentiment of the universal Church that the intercession of Mary is not only useful, but even necessary to obtain graces. The Church devoutly applies these scriptural quotations to Mary: "In me is all hope of life and virtue. Come to me all you who desire me" (Si 24:25). "Blessed is the man who hears me and who watches daily at my gate and waits at my doorposts" (Pr 8:34). "He who finds me finds life and shall have salvation from the Lord" (Pr 8:35). It is not without reason that Holy Church salutes her with "Hail, our hope!"

St. Bernard says, "Let us then seek for graces and seek them through Mary" (*Sermon "On the Aqueduct"*). If we ask for graces without her intercession we shall be making an effort to fly without wings and we shall obtain nothing.

We can read often of the many favors Mary has granted, by her intercession with her Son and her Lord, to people who have visited her shrines, especially in the parish churches.

For St. Albert the Great she obtained such wisdom that he

became a world renowned theologian. St. John Berchmans testified to the great graces he obtained through her in a chapel of the Jesuits' Roman college. St. Bernardine of Siena became the greatest preacher of his time in Italy through skills granted through her intercession.

It is always wise, therefore, to join a visit to Mary to your daily visit to the Blessed Sacrament. If you do this with tender affection and confidence you may hope to receive great things from this most gracious Lady who always bestows great gifts on those who offer her even the least act of homage.

> *Mary, Queen of sweetest hope,*
> *Who can e'er forget thee?*
> *By thy mercy, by thy love,*
> *Have pity, Queen, on me!*

III.

Spiritual Communion

(Since in the time of St. Alphonsus it was rare for the laity to receive daily Holy Communion even if they attended daily Mass, the saint puts great stress on spiritual Communion as a substitute.)

A spiritual Communion is a very salutary practice each time one visits the Most Blessed Sacrament. A spiritual Communion, according to St. Thomas Aquinas, consists in an ardent desire to receive Jesus in the Most Holy Sacrament and in lovingly embracing him as if we had actually received him.

St. Peter Faber, the first companion of St. Ignatius in the Society of Jesus, recommended spiritual Communion as of the highest utility in preparing to receive sacramental Communion.

An example of an Act of Spiritual Communion

> My Jesus, I believe that You are truly present in the Most Blessed Sacrament. I love You above all things and I desire to possess You within my soul. Since I am unable now to receive You sacramentally, come at least spiritually into my heart. I embrace You as being already there and unite myself wholly and entirely to You; never permit me to be separated from You. Amen.

IV.

Manner of Making the Visit

A. VISIT TO THE BLESSED SACRAMENT

Preliminary Prayer: My Lord Jesus Christ, because of the love You have for us, You remain night and day in this Sacrament full of compassion and love, awaiting, calling, and welcoming all who visit You.

I believe that You are present in the Sacrament of the Altar; I adore You from the abyss of my nothingness and I thank You for all the graces You have bestowed on me, and in particular for having given me Yourself in this Sacrament; for having given me Your most holy Mother Mary for my advocate and for having called me to visit You in this church.

I now salute Your most loving Heart, and this for three ends:

1. In thanksgiving for this great gift;
2. To make amends to You for all the outrages which You receive in this Sacrament from all Your enemies;
3. I intend by this visit to adore You in all places on earth in

which You are present in this Sacrament and in which You are the least revered and the most abandoned.

My Jesus, I love You with my whole heart. I grieve for having so many times offended Your infinite goodness. I am determined, with the help of Your grace, never to offend You again.

Now, miserable and unworthy though I be, I consecrate myself to You without reserve. I give You and renounce my entire will, my affections, my desires and all that I possess. From now on, dispose of me and all I have at Your pleasure. All I ask of You and desire is Your holy love, final perseverance, and the perfect accomplishment of Your will.

I recommend to You the souls in purgatory, especially those who had the most devotion to the Most Blessed Sacrament and to the Most Blessed Virgin Mary. I also recommend to You all poor sinners.

Finally, my dear Savior, I unite all my affections with the affections of Your most loving Heart, and I offer them, thus united, to Your Eternal Father and beg him, in Your name, to accept and grant them. Amen.

An Act of Spiritual Communion: My Jesus, I believe that You are truly present in the Most Blessed Sacrament. I love You above all things and I desire to possess You within my soul. Since I am unable to receive You sacramentally at this time, come at least spiritually into my heart. I embrace You as being already there and unite myself entirely to You. Never permit me to be separated from You. Amen.

A Shorter Act: I believe that You, O Jesus, are present in the Most Holy Sacrament. I love You and desire You. Come into my heart. I embrace You. Never leave me. Amen.

Prayers or readings of one's choice.

Prayerful Aspirations: "May the burning and most sweet power of Your love, O Lord Jesus Christ, absorb my mind that I may die through love of Your love, who was graciously pleased to die through love of my love." St. Francis of Assisi.

"O love not loved! O love not known!" St. Mary Magdalene de Pazzi.

"O my friend, when will You take me to Yourself!" St. Peter of Alcantara.

B. VISIT TO THE BLESSED VIRGIN

Readings or prayers of one's choice.

Closing Prayer: Most holy Immaculate Virgin and my Mother Mary, you are the Mother of my Lord and Queen of the World, the advocate, the hope, the refuge of sinners, I have recourse to you today, I who am the most miserable of all.

I bring you my most humble homage, O great Queen, and I thank you for all the gifts you have conferred on me until now, particularly for having saved me from the hell which I have so often deserved.

I love you, O most amiable Lady, and for the love which I give you I promise to serve you always and to do all in my power to make others love you also. I place all my hope in you; I confide my salvation into your care.

Accept me as your servant and receive me under your mantle, O Mother of mercy. Since you are so powerful with God, deliver me from all temptations, or rather, obtain for me the strength to triumph over them until death.

I ask for a perfect love for Jesus Christ. Through your intercession I hope to die a happy death. O my Mother, by the love which you have for God, I beg you to help me at all times but especially at the last moment of my life.

Leave me not, I beg you, until you see me safe in heaven, blessing you and singing your mercies for all eternity. Amen. So I hope. So may it be.

Book Three

Meditations for Corpus Christi

I.

The Love of Jesus in the Most Holy Sacrament

Our most loving Redeemer, knowing that he must leave this earth and return to his Father as soon as he had accomplished the work of our redemption by his death, and seeing that the hour of his death had now come — "Jesus knew that his hour had come to pass from this world to the Father" (Jn 13:1) — would not leave us alone in this valley of tears, so what did he do?

He instituted the Most Holy Sacrament of the Eucharist in which he left us his whole self.

"No tongue," said St. Peter of Alcantara, "is able to declare the greatness of the love that Jesus bears for every soul. Therefore, this Spouse when he would leave this earth, in order that his absence might not cause us to forget him, left us as a memorial this Blessed Sacrament in which he himself remained. He did not want any other pledge to keep alive our remembrance of him than he himself."

Jesus would not be separated from us by his death. He instituted this Sacrament of love in order to be with us even to the end of the world. "Behold I am with you always until the end of the age" (Mt 28:20).

See him, then, as faith teaches us. See him on so many altars shut up as in so many prisons of love so that he may be found by everyone who seeks him. "But, O Lord," St. Bernard objects, "this does not become Your majesty." Jesus Christ answers, "It is enough that it becomes my love."

They feel great tenderness and devotion who go to Jerusalem

and visit the cave where the Incarnate Word was born, the hall where he was scourged, the hill of Calvary on which he died and the sepulchre where he was buried. How much greater ought our devotion be when we visit a tabernacle in which Jesus himself remains in the Most Holy Sacrament.

John of Avila used to say that of all the sanctuaries and shrines there is not one to be found more excellent and devout than a church where Jesus is sacramentally present.

(The meditation should be followed by prayers and affections, and a visit to Mary.)

II.

Jesus Remains on the Altar
So That Everyone May Be Able to Find Him

St. Teresa said that in this world it is impossible for all subjects to speak to the king. As for the poor, the most they can hope for is to speak with him through a third party.

But to speak to the King of Heaven there is no need of a third party. Anyone who wishes to speak to him can find him directly in the Most Holy Sacrament and can speak to him at any time and without restraint

For this reason, she adds, Jesus Christ has concealed his majesty in the Blessed Sacrament, under the appearance of bread, in order to give us more confidence and to take away all fear of approaching him.

Jesus continually seems to exclaim from the altar, "Come to me all you who labor are heavily burdened and I will refresh you" (Mt 11:28). Come, he says to the poor, the weak, the afflicted; come he says to the just and to sinners. You shall find in me a remedy for your losses and afflictions.

Such is the desire of Jesus: to console anyone who has recourse to him. He remains day and night on our altars that he may be easily found by all and that he may bestow favors on everyone.

The saints experienced this in such a mighty way that days and nights before the Blessed Sacrament seemed like moments. Were you to ask them what they do in the presence of their sacramental Lord they would reply, "I give thanks, I love, I pray." St. Philip Neri used the aspiration, "Behold my love, behold all my love." If Jesus were thus our whole love, days and nights in his presence would seem like moments to us as well.

III.

The Great Gift Which Jesus Has Made Us by Giving Himself to Us in the Blessed Sacrament

The love of Jesus Christ was not satisfied with sacrificing for us his divine life in the midst of a sea of ignominies and torments in order to prove to us that affection he had for us. Beyond that, in order to invite our love more generously, on the night before he died he left us his whole self as our food in the Holy Eucharist.

God is omnipotent, but after he has given himself to a soul in this Sacrament, he has nothing more to give. The Council of Trent says that Jesus, in giving himself to us in Holy Communion, pours forth, as it were, all the riches of his infinite love towards men and women (Sess. 13, c.2).

How would that vassal esteem himself honored, writes St. Francis de Sales, were his prince, while at table, to send a portion of his own dish. Jesus in Holy Communion gives us our food, not only a portion of his own meal but all of his sacred flesh: "Take and eat, this is My Body" (Mt 26:26).

Together with his body he gives us also his soul and his divinity. St. John Chrysostom says that our Lord, in giving himself to us in the Blessed Sacrament gives us all that he has, and nothing remains for him to give us.

O wonderful prodigy of divine love, that God, who is the Lord of all, makes himself entirely ours!

IV.

The Great Love Which Jesus Has Shown Us in the Blessed Sacrament

"Jesus knew that his hour had come to pass from this world to the Father, He loved his own in the world and he loved them to the end" (Jn 13:1). Jesus, knowing that the hour of his death was come, desired to leave us, before he died, the greatest pledge of his affection that he could give us. This was the gift of the Most Holy Sacrament.

He loved us with the greatest love with which he could love us, by giving us his whole self. And note the time at which Jesus instituted this great Sacrament in which he left himself. On the night preceding his death: "For I received from the Lord, what I also handed on to you, that the Lord Jesus, on the night he was handed over, took bread and after he had given thanks broke it and said, 'This is my body that is for you'" (1 Cor 11:23).

At the very time that men were preparing to put him to death he gave them this last proof of his love. The marks of affection that we receive from our friends at the time of their death remain more deeply impressed on our hearts. This is the reason why Jesus bestowed on us this gift of the Blessed Sacrament just before his death.

With what good reason, therefore, St. Thomas Aquinas calls

this gift "a sacrament and a pledge of love." St. Bernard calls it "the love of loves" because in this Sacrament Jesus Christ united and accomplished all the other acts of love which he had shown us. St. Mary Magdalene de Pazzi called the day on which Jesus instituted this Sacrament "the day of love."

V.

The Union of the Soul with Jesus in Holy Communion

Dionysius the Areopagite says that the principal effect of love is to tend to union. It was for this very purpose that Jesus instituted Holy Communion that he might unite himself entirely to our souls. He had given himself to us as our master, our example and our victim.

It only remained for him to give himself to us as our food that he might become one with us, as food becomes one with the person who eats it. The wonder is that here we become one with the Food. This he did by instituting the Sacrament of love.

"The highest degree of love," says St. Bernardine of Siena, "is when he gave himself to us to be our food. He who gave himself to be united with us in every way as food and he who takes it are mutually united."

Jesus Christ was not satisfied with only uniting himself to our human nature, but he would, by this Sacrament, find a way of uniting himself to each one of us so that he himself would be wholly united with the one who receives him.

St. Francis de Sales observes, in the *Introduction to the Devout Life* (2:21), "In no other action can our Savior be considered more tender or more loving than in this in which he, as it were, annihilates himself and reduces himself to food that he may penetrate our souls and unite himself to the hearts of his faithful."

Because Jesus loved us so ardently, he desired to unite himself to us in the Holy Eucharist in order that we might become the same thing with him. St. John Chrysostom teaches that he mingled himself with us so that we might be one; this belongs to those who love greatly. St. Lawrence Justinian adds that Christ willed that we should have one heart with him.

Jesus himself said, "Whoever eats my flesh and drinks my blood remains in me and I in him" (Jn. 6:56). Therefore whoever receives Holy Communion abides in Jesus and Jesus abides in him. The union is not merely of affection or love but it is a true and real union. In commenting on this passage, St. Cyril of Alexandria observes that as two wax tapers when melted unite themselves to each other so the one who receives Holy Communion becomes one with Jesus Christ.

Whenever we receive Holy Communion, let us imagine Christ saying to us, "See, beloved friend, the beautiful union between me and you. Come then, let us remain constantly united in love and never be separated from one another."

VI.

Jesus Christ Desires to Unite Himself with Us

Jesus, knowing that his hour had come (cf. Jn 13:1) called it "his hour" because it was the time for him to begin his Passion. Why was so sad an hour such an important hour? Because this was the hour toward which his whole life was directed. He had determined to leave us the Holy Eucharist at this most solemn hour.

He desired to be united entirely with those for whom he was about to give his blood, his life. "I have eagerly desired to eat this Passover with you before I suffer" (Lk 22:15). This is how he expressed the ardor of his desire to be united with us in Holy

Communion. These words which came from the Heart of Jesus give voice to the most ardent charity.

Now the same flame which burnt in the Heart of Christ then, burns there at present as he gives the same invitation to all of us today to receive him as did those privileged disciples at the Last Supper: "Take and eat; this is my body" (Mt 26:26).

To encourage us even more strongly, he promises Paradise to us. "Whoever eats my flesh and drinks my blood has eternal life" (Jn 6:54). And to those who refuse? "Unless you eat the flesh of the Son of Man and drink his blood, you do not have life within you" (Jn 6:53).

These invitations, promises, and admonitions all arise from the desire of Jesus Christ to unite himself to us in Holy Communion through the love that he bears us. St. Mechtilde was told in vision, "There is not a bee which seeks the honey out of flowers with such eagerness of delight as I have to enter into souls that desire me."

Jesus, because he loves us, desires to be loved by us; because he desires us he wants us to desire him. As St. Gregory puts it, "God thirsts to be thirsted after." Blessed is that soul who approaches Holy Communion with a great desire to be united to Jesus Christ.

VII.

Holy Communion Obtains Perseverance in Divine Grace for Us

When Jesus comes to the soul in Holy Communion he brings every grace to it, especially the grace of holy perseverance. This is the principal effect of the Most Holy Sacrament — to nourish the soul that receives it with this food of life, to give it great strength to advance to perfection and to resist those enemies who desire our death.

Jesus calls himself in this Sacrament heavenly bread. "I am the living bread that came down from heaven; whoever eats this bread will live forever. And the bread that I give is my flesh for the life of the world" (Jn 6:51). Even as earthly bread sustains the life of the body, so this heavenly bread sustains the life of the soul by making it persevere in the grace of God.

The Council of Trent teaches that Holy Communion is that remedy which delivers us from daily faults and preserves us from mortal sin (Sess. 13, c.2). Pope Innocent III wrote that Jesus Christ by his Passion delivers us from sins committed and by Holy Communion from sins which we might commit.

St. Bonaventure points out that sinners must not keep away from Communion because they have been sinners; on the contrary, for this very reason they ought to receive it more frequently because "the more infirm a person feels himself to be, the more he is in want of a physician."

VIII.

Preparation for Communion and Thanksgiving After It

Why does it happen that so many souls, after so many Communions make so little advance in the way of God? The fault is not in the food but in the disposition of the person who eats it. That is to say in the want of due preparation on the part of the communicant.

Fire soon burns dry wood but not that which is green because the latter is not fit to burn. The saints derived great profit from their Communions because they were very careful in their preparation for it.

There are two principal things which we should do to prepare ourselves for Holy Communion to derive the greatest fruit.

The first is detachment from creatures by driving from our heart everything that is not of God and for God. Although the soul may be in the state of grace if the heart is so occupied by earthly affections that there is more of earth than divine love there, then there is no room to grow in divine love.

The second thing that is necessary in order to reap the greatest fruit from Communion is the desire to receive Jesus Christ with the view of loving him more. At this banquet none are satiated but those who feel great hunger. St. Francis de Sales recommends that the principal intention in receiving Communion should be to advance in the love of God.

It is also necessary to make a thanksgiving after Communion. There is no prayer more dear to God than that which is made after Holy Communion. We must occupy this time in acts of love and prayers. The devout acts of love which we make have greater merit in the sight of God than those which we make at any other time because they are then animated by the presence of Jesus Christ who is united to our souls.

St. Teresa says that Jesus, after Communion, remains in the soul as on a throne of grace and says to the communicant, "What would you have me do for you? I have come from heaven on purpose to grant you graces. Ask what you will, as much as you will, and you will be heard."

Oh, what great treasures of grace do they lose who pray but a short time to God after Holy Communion!

Book Four

Novena to the Sacred Heart

Introduction

(This pamphlet was written in 1758.)

The devotion of all devotions is love for Jesus Christ and frequent meditation on the love which this amiable Redeemer has borne and still bears for us.

Many people multiply their devotions but neglect this one. Many preachers deliver learned homilies but overlook this most important one. Love for Jesus Christ should be the principal, if not the only, devotion of a Christian. It should be the chief object of preachers and confessors, that they recommend to their listeners and penitents the devotion to the love of Jesus. They should help inflame their listeners' hearts with the love of Jesus Christ.

Neglect of this devotion is the reason why souls make so little progress in virtue and retain their same faults and defects. They may even fall back into grievous sin if they are not taught to acquire and grow in the love of Jesus Christ which is that golden cord which unites and binds the soul to God.

For this sole purpose did the Eternal Word come into this world, to make himself loved. "I have come to set the earth on fire and how I wish it were already blazing!" (Lk 12:49). This is why the Eternal Father sent him into the world, in order that he might make known to us his love and so obtain ours in return.

He proclaims that he will love us in the same proportion as we love Jesus Christ: "For the Father himself loves you because you have loved me and have come to believe that I came from God" (Jn 16:27). Moreover he gives us his graces as far as we ask for them in the name

53

of his Son: "Whatever you ask the Father in my name he will give you" (Jn 16:23).

Furthermore, we come to eternal beatitude only in so far as he finds us conformable to the life of Jesus Christ. "For those he foreknew he also predestined to be conformed to the image of his Son" (Rm 8:29). We shall never acquire this conformity, nor even ever desire it, if we are not attentive to meditating on the love which Jesus Christ bore for us.

To St. Margaret Mary Alacoque, a nun of the Visitation Order, our Savior revealed his wish that the devotion and the feast of his Sacred Heart should be established and propagated in the Church. This he desired so that devout souls should, by their adoration and prayer, make reparation for the injuries his heart constantly receives from the ungrateful when he is exposed in the Sacrament of the Altar.

St. Margaret Mary also records a vision in which, while at prayer before the Blessed Sacrament, Jesus Christ showed her his heart surrounded by thorns, with the cross on the top and in a throne of flames.

He said to her, "Behold the heart which has so loved mankind and has spared nothing for love of them, even to consuming itself to give them the pledges of its love, but which receives from the majority no other recompense but ingratitude and insults towards the Sacrament of love. What grieves me most is that so many of them are consecrated to me."

Then he desired her to use whatever efforts she could to get a special feast in honor of his divine heart. He gave three reasons:

1. That the faithful should give thanks to him for the great gift he has left them in the adorable Eucharist;
2. That loving souls should make amends by their prayers and love for the irreverence and insults which he has received and still receives from sinners in this Most Holy Sacrament;
3. That they should also make up for the honor which he does not receive in so many churches where he is so little adored and reverenced.

He promised that he would make the riches of his Sacred Heart abound towards those who should render him honor both on the feast day and on every other day when they should visit him in the Most Holy Sacrament.

This devotion to the Sacred Heart of Jesus Christ is nothing more than an exercise of love towards this amiable Savior. As to the principal object of this devotion, the spiritual subject is the love with which the heart of Jesus Christ is inflamed towards mankind, because love is generally attributed to the heart, as we read in many places of Scripture: "My son, give me your heart" (Pr 23:26); "My heart and my flesh cry out for the living God" (Ps 84:3); "Though my heart and my flesh waste away, God is the rock of my heart and my portion forever" (Ps 73:26); "The love of God has been poured out into our hearts through the Holy Spirit that has been given to us" (Rm 5:5).

The material or sensible object is the most Sacred Heart of Jesus, not taken separately by itself, but united to his sacred humanity and consequently to the divine Person of the Word.

I.

The Amiable Heart of Jesus

He who shows himself amiable in everything must necessarily make himself loved. Oh, if we only applied ourselves to discover all the good qualities by which Jesus Christ renders himself worthy of our love, we should all be under the happy necessity of loving him. What heart among all hearts can be found more worthy of love than the Sacred Heart of Jesus?

A heart all pure, all holy, and all full of love towards God and towards us, because all its desires are only for the divine glory and our good — this is the heart in which God finds all his delight.

Every perfection, every virtue reigns in this heart — a most ardent love for God, his Father, united to the greatest humility and respect that can possibly exist; a sovereign concern for our sins which he has taken upon himself, united to the extreme confidence of a most affectionate Son; a sovereign abhorrence for our sins, united to a lively compassion for our miseries; an extreme sorrow, united to a perfect conformity to the will of God.

In Jesus is found everything that can be most amiable. Some are attracted to love others by their beauty, by their innocence, by living with them, or by devotion. But if there were a person in whom all of these and other virtues were united, who could help loving him?

If some hero existed in whom all these qualities were present to the fullest degree, could we help but love and admire him? How is it possible, then, that Jesus Christ, who possesses in himself all these virtues and in the most perfect degree and who loves us so tenderly — how is it possible that he should be so little loved by us. He should be the prime object of our love.

O my God, how is it that Jesus, who alone is worthy of love and who has given us so many proofs of the love that he bears us, should be alone, as it were, the unlucky one with us, who cannot arrive at making us love him; as if he were not sufficiently worthy of our love!

No wonder saints like Rose of Lima, Catherine of Genoa, Teresa and Mary Magdalene de Pazzi shed copious tears, with exclamations like: "Love is not loved! Love is not loved!"

(Each meditation should then proceed with affections and prayers, and conclude with a short visit to the Blessed Mother.)

II.

The Loving Heart of Jesus

Oh, if we could but understand the love that burns in the heart of Jesus for us! He has loved us so much that if all men and women, all the angels and all the saints were to unite, with all their energies, they could not arrive at a millionth part of the love that Jesus bears us. He loves us infinitely more than we love ourselves.

He has loved us even to excess: "And behold two men were conversing with him, Moses and Elijah, who appeared in glory and spoke of his exodus that he was going to accomplish in Jerusalem" (Lk 9:30-31). What greater excess of love could there be than for God to die for his creatures?

He has loved us to the greatest degree: "He loved his own in the world and he loved them to the end" (Jn 13:1). After having loved us from eternity — for there never was a moment from eternity when God did not think of us and did not love each one of us, "With age-old love I have loved you" (Jr 31:3) — for love of us he made himself man and chose a life of suffering and death on the cross for our sake.

Is this not an excess of love to stupefy with astonishment the angels of paradise for all eternity?

This love has induced him also to remain with us in the Holy Sacrament as on a throne of love. He remains there under the appearance of a small piece of bread, shut up in a ciborium, seemingly in an annihilation of his majesty, without movement or the use of his senses so that it seems that he performs no other office than that of loving men and women.

Love makes us desire the constant presence of the one we love. It is this love and this desire that makes Jesus Christ reside with us in the Most Holy Sacrament. It seems too short a time to this loving Savior to have been only thirty-three years with us on earth; therefore, to show his desire of being constantly with us he thought it right to perform the greatest of all miracles in the institution of the Holy Eucharist.

The work of redemption was already completed; we had already become reconciled to God. For what purpose then did Jesus remain on earth in this Sacrament? He remains there because he cannot bear to separate himself from us, as he has said that he takes delight in his sons and daughters.

This love has induced him to become even food for our souls so as to unite himself to us and to make his heart and ours as one. "Whoever eats my flesh and drinks my blood remains in me and I in him" (Jn 6:56). Oh excess of divine love!

If anything could shake my faith in the Eucharist it would not be the doubt as to how the bread could become flesh or how Jesus could be in several places at once and confined in so small a space, because I would answer that God can do everything.

But if I ask myself how he could love us so much as to make himself our food, I can only answer but that this is a mystery of faith beyond my comprehension and that the love of Jesus cannot be understood, so great it is.

O Love of Jesus, make yourself known to us and make us love you!

(Affections, prayers and visit to Mary.)

III.

The Heart of Jesus Desiring to Be Loved

Jesus has no need of us. He is equally happy, equally rich, equally powerful with or without our love. Yet, as St. Thomas Aquinas points out, he loves us as if his happiness depended on our love: "What is man that you make much of him or pay him any heed? (Job 7:17), "What is man that you should be mindful of him or the son of man that you should care for him?" (Ps 8:5).

With what eagerness God desires and asks for our love. It would have been a great enough favor if God had only permitted us to love him. The princes of this earth do not desire the love of their subjects; the King of Heaven, Jesus Christ, is he who earnestly demands our love: "You shall love the Lord your God with all your heart, with all your soul and with all your mind" (Mt 22:37).

He asks it outright: "My son, give me your heart" (Pr 23:26). If he is driven from a soul, he does not depart but stands outside the door of the heart and he calls and knocks to be let in: "Behold, I stand at the door and knock" (Rv 3:20). Indeed, he is insistent: "I heard my lover knocking: 'Open to me my sister, my beloved!'" (Sg 5:2).

In short, he takes delight in being loved by us and is quite happy when a soul says to him and repeats it often, "My God, my God, I love you."

All this is the effect of the great love he bears us. He who loves, necessarily desires to be loved. The heart requires the heart; love seeks love. In commenting on the Song of Songs, St. Bernard says, "Why does God love but that he might be loved himself?"

But God himself said it first: "What does the Lord your God ask of you but to fear the Lord your God and follow his ways exactly, to love and to serve the Lord your God with all your heart and with all your soul?" (Dt 10:12).

Therefore he tells us that he is the Shepherd who, having found the lost sheep, calls all the others to rejoice with him: "Rejoice with me because I have found my lost sheep" (Lk 15:6). He is also that Father who, when his lost son returns and throws himself at his feet, not only forgives but embraces him tenderly.

He warns that those who do not love him are condemned to spiritual death: "Whoever does not love remains in death" (1 Jn 3:14). On the contrary he reminds us that those who love him he will keep in his love: "God is love and whoever remains in love remains in God and God in him" (1 Jn 4:16).

Oh that such invitations, such entreaties, such threats and such promises might move us to love God who so much desires to be loved!

(Affections, prayers, visit to Mary)

IV.

The Sorrowful Heart of Jesus

It is impossible to consider how deeply the heart of Jesus was afflicted for us and not feel pity for him. He himself tells us that his heart was overwhelmed with such sorrow that this alone would have been sufficient to take his life and make him die of pure grief if the power of his divinity had not, by a miracle, prevented such a death: "My soul is sorrowful even to death" (Mk 14:34).

The principal sorrow which afflicted the heart of Jesus so much was not the sight of the torments and infamy which men were preparing for him, but the sight of their ingratitude towards his immense love.

He distinctly foresaw all the sins which we would commit after all his sufferings and such a bitter and ignominious death. He foresaw, especially, the horrible insults which men would offer to his adorable heart, which he has left us in the Most Holy Sacrament as a proof of his love.

O my God, what affronts has not Jesus Christ received from us in this Sacrament of Love? One has trampled him underfoot, another has thrown him into the gutters, others have availed themselves of him to pay homage to the devil!

Yet the sight of all these insults did not prevent him from leaving us this great pledge of his love. He has a sovereign hatred of sin but still it seems as if his love for us had overcome the hatred he bore for sin since he was content to permit these sacrileges rather than to deprive souls that love him of this divine food. Shouldn't this be enough to make us love a heart that has loved us so much?

Hasn't Jesus Christ done enough to deserve our love? Ungrateful that we are, shall we still leave Jesus forsaken on the altar as so many do? We should unite with all those who do acknowledge his Presence and join with them in their acts of love. The heart of Jesus remains in the tabernacle burning with love for us and shall we not, in his Presence, burn with love for Jesus?

(Affections, prayers and a visit to Mary)

V.

The Compassionate Heart of Jesus

Where shall we ever find a heart more compassionate or tender than the heart of Jesus, or one that had a greater feeling for our miseries?

This pity induced him to descend from Heaven to this earth; it made him say that he was that Good Shepherd who came to give his life to save his sheep. In order to obtain the pardon for our sins he would not spare himself, but would sacrifice himself on the Cross, that by his sufferings he might satisfy for the chastisement we have deserved.

This pity and compassion makes him say even now: "Why should you die, O house of Israel? For I have no pleasure in the death of anyone who dies, says the Lord God. Return and live!" (Ezk 18:31-32).

O my poor children, he says, why will you damn yourselves by abandoning me? Don't you see that by separating yourselves from me you are hastening to eternal death? I desire not to see you lost. Do not despair; as often as you wish to return, return, and you shall recover your life. "Return and live!"

This compassion even makes him say that he is that loving Father who, though he sees himself despised by his son, yet, if that son returns a penitent, he cannot reject him but embraces him tenderly and forgets all the injuries he has received: "None of the crimes he committed shall be remembered against him" (Ezk 18:22).

This is not the way men behave. They may forgive, but they

retain the remembrance of the offense received and feel inclined still to avenge themselves. And even if they refrain from taking revenge because they fear the Lord, they always feel a repugnance in the presence of persons who have vilified them.

O my Jesus, you pardon penitent sinners and give them everything in Holy Communion both in this life and in the next. Where, then, is there to be found a heart so amiable and compassionate as Yours, O my dearest Savior!

(Affections, prayers, visit to Mary)

VI.

The Generous Heart of Jesus

It is characteristic of good-hearted people to desire to make everybody happy and especially those most distressed and afflicted. But who can ever find anyone who has a better heart than Jesus Christ? He is infinite goodness and has therefore a sovereign desire to communicate his riches to us. "With me are riches and honor, enduring wealth and prosperity . . . Granting wealth to those who love me and fulfilling their treasuries" (Pr 8:18, 21).

For this purpose he made himself poor, as the Apostle says, that he might make us rich: "For your sake he became poor though he was rich, so that by his poverty you might become rich" (2 Cor 8:9).

For this purpose, also, he chose to remain with us in the Most Holy Sacrament where he remains constantly with his hands full of graces to dispense them to those who come to visit him. For this reason he gives himself wholly to us in Holy Communion, giving us to understand from this that he cannot refuse us any good gifts since he even gives himself to us entirely: "He who did not spare his own Son but handed him over for us all, how will he not also give us everything else along with him?" (Rm 8:32).

In the heart of Jesus we receive every good, every grace we desire, "that in him you were enriched in every way . . . so that you are not lacking in any spiritual gift" (1 Cor 1:5, 8). We must understand then that we are debtors to the heart of Jesus for all the graces we have received — graces of redemption, of vocation, of light, of pardon, the grace to resist temptation and to bear patiently with contradictions. Without his assistance we could not do anything good: "Without me you can do nothing" (Jn 15:5).

Our Savior reminds us that if we have not received more graces we should not complain but blame ourselves who have neglected to ask for them: "Until now you have not asked anything in my name; ask and receive so that your joy may be complete" (Jn 16:24).

Oh how rich and liberal is the heart of Jesus towards everyone who has recourse to him! "Enriching all who call upon him," as the Apostle puts it (Rm 10:12). Oh what great mercies do those souls receive who are in earnest in asking help of Jesus Christ: "For you, O Lord, are good and forgiving, abounding in kindness to all who call upon you" (Ps 86:5).

Let us, therefore, always go to this heart and ask with confidence and we shall obtain all we want.

(Affections, prayers, visit to Mary)

VII.

The Grateful Heart of Jesus

The heart of Jesus is so grateful that it cannot behold the most trifling works done for the love of him — our smallest word spoken for his glory, a single thought directed towards pleasing him — without giving to each its own reward. He is so grateful that he always returns a hundredfold: "You shall receive a hundredfold" (Mt 19:29).

When we are grateful we give recompense on a one-for-one basis and consider ourselves relieved of further obligation. Jesus Christ does not do it this way with us. Not only is there the hundredfold in this life but it continues on in eternity. Would we not be extremely foolish not to do as much as we can to please this most grateful heart?

But, in reality, how do most people try to please Jesus Christ? How can they be so ungrateful to our Savior. How they overlook him and neglect him!

If he had only shed a single drop of his precious blood, or one tear alone for our salvation, yet would we be under infinite obligation to him. This drop, this tear would have been of infinite value in the sight of God towards obtaining for us every grace.

But Jesus employed every moment of his life for us. He has given us all his merits, all his sufferings, all his ignominies, all his blood and his life. Therefore we are under not one but infinite obligations to love him.

Look how we treat our pets. When they show signs of affection towards us, we feel constrained to respond with affection. How then can we be so ungrateful towards God. His gifts and favors go on without end but instead of gratitude, so many people meet them with offenses and negligence.

O Lord, enlighten these ungrateful ones so that they may know the love you have for them.

(*Affections, prayers, visit to Mary*)

VIII.

The Despised Heart of Jesus

There is no greater sorrow for a heart that loves than to see its love despised. That ingratitude is so much the more when the proofs given of this love have been so great.

If every human being were to renounce all his goods, go and live in the desert, feed himself on herbs, macerate himself with penances, and at last give himself up to be murdered for Christ's sake, what recompense could he render for the life, the sufferings, the blood that this great Son of God has given for all?

If we were to sacrifice ourselves every moment, even unto death, we should certainly not recompense in the smallest degree the love that Jesus Christ has shown us by giving himself to us in the Most Holy Sacrament. Only conceive that God should conceal himself under the species of bread to become the food of one of his creatures.

But what recompense and gratitude do people render to Jesus Christ? What but ill-treatment, contempt of his laws and maxims — injuries such as they would not commit towards their enemy or the greatest villain on earth. Can we think of all these injuries which Jesus Christ has received and still receives and not feel sorrow for them?

Should we not endeavor, by our love, to recompense the infinite love of his divine heart which remains in the Most Holy Sacrament, inflamed with the same love towards us and anxious to communicate and to impart to us every good gift and to give himself entirely to us, ever ready to receive us into his heart whenever we go to him? "I will not reject anyone who comes to me" (Jn 6:37).

We have been accustomed to hear of the Creation, Incarnation, Redemption, of Jesus born in a stable, of Jesus dead on the Cross. If some other person had conferred on us any of these benefits, we could not help loving him. It seems that God alone has, so to say, this bad luck with people, that, although he has done his utmost to make them love him, yet he cannot attain this end, and, instead of being loved he sees himself despised and neglected.

All this arises from the forgetfulness of men and women of the love of God.

(Affections, prayers, visit to Mary)

IX.

The Faithful Heart of Jesus

Oh how faithful is the loving heart of Jesus towards those whom he calls to his love: "The one who calls you is faithful, and he will also accomplish it" (1 Th 5:24).

The faithfulness of God gives us confidence to hope all things, though we deserve nothing. If we have driven God from our heart, let us open the door to him and he will immediately enter according to the promise he has made: "Behold, I stand at the door and knock. If anyone hears my voice and opens the door, I will enter his house and dine with him" (Rv 3:20).

If we wish for graces, let us ask God for them in the name of Jesus Christ, and he has promised us that we shall obtain them: "Whatever you ask the Father in my name he will give you" (Jn 16:23).

If we are tempted, let us trust in his merits and he will not permit our enemies to strive with us beyond our strength: "God is faithful and will not let you be tried beyond your strength" (1 Cor 10:13).

Oh how much better it is to deal with God than with men! How often do men promise and then fail to deliver either because they lie in making promises or because, after having promised, they change their minds. "God is not man that he should speak falsely, nor human, that he should change his mind" (Nb 23:19).

God cannot be unfaithful to his promises because, being truth itself, he cannot lie; nor can he change his mind, because all that he wills is just and right. He has promised to receive all who come to him, to give help to all who ask, to love all who love him. Shall he not do it then? "Is he one to speak and not act, to decree and not fulfill?" (Nb 23:19).

Oh that we were as faithful with God as he is with us! How often have we, in times past, promised him to be his, to serve him and love him, and then have betrayed him, and renouncing his service have sold ourselves as slaves of the devil.

Let us beg him to give us the strength to be faithful to him for the future. How blessed we shall be if we are faithful to Jesus Christ in the few things that he asks us to do! He will, indeed, be faithful in remunerating us with infinitely great rewards. We will hear him declare: "Well done, my good and faithful servant. Since you were faithful in small matters, I will give you great responsibilities. Come, share your master's joy" (Mt 25:21).

(*Affections, prayers, visit to Mary*)

Affections of Love Towards the Heart of Jesus

(This was found among the Saint's papers but not published until 1875, almost a century after his death.)

O amiable Heart of my Savior! You are the seat of all virtues, the source of all graces, the burning furnace in which all souls are inflamed. You are the object of all God's love; you are the refuge of the afflicted and the dwelling place of the souls that love you.

O heart worthy of reigning over all hearts and of possessing the affection of all hearts! O heart that was wounded for me on the Cross by the lance of my sins, and that remains afterwards continually wounded for me on the altar in the Blessed Sacrament, but not by any other lance than that of the love you have for me!

O loving heart that loves us with such tenderness and yet is so little loved in return. Remedy such great ingratitude by inflaming our hearts with a true love for you. Would that I could go around the whole world to make known the graces, the sweetness, the treasures you give to those who truly love you!

Accept the desire I have of seeing all hearts burn with love for you. O divine heart, be my consolation in trials, my rest in labors, my comfort in anxiety, my haven from stress.

I consecrate to you my body and my soul, my heart and my life, together with all that I am. I unite all my thoughts, all my affections and all my desires to yours.

Oh! eternal Father, I offer you the pure love of the heart of Jesus. If you reject my love, you cannot reject those of your Son who is sanctity itself. Let that supply what is lacking in me and make me pleasing in your eyes. Amen.

St. Catherine of Genoa was one day permitted to see the heart of Jesus in his chest, and she saw it all on fire.

One day our Lord appeared to St. Mechtilde, and she heard the heart of Jesus beating violently, as if someone had struck him on the chest. The Lord told her that his heart had been beating like this since his infancy on account of the love with which it was inflamed for the whole human race.

He also told her, "My love for souls is just the same as the love which I bore them at the time of my Passion. I would die as many times as there are souls to be saved."

Jesus said to St. Gertrude, "If it were expedient, I would offer for you alone what I have suffered for the whole world."

St. Carpus appeared to be ready to consign all the souls of sinners to the deep abyss. Jesus said to him, "For my part, O Carpus, I am still ready to allow myself to be crucified for mankind."

St. John of the Cross said, "Jesus loves each one of us as much as he loves the whole human race."

Book Five

The Practice of the Love of Jesus Christ

Introduction

(This booklet was published in 1768 and became one of the best known and most wide-spread of the works of St. Alphonsus. It is, in effect, his exposition of the famous 13th chapter of 1 Corinthians on love, the greatest gift [1 Cor 13:13].)

A. HOW DESERVING JESUS CHRIST IS OF OUR LOVE ON ACCOUNT OF THE LOVE HE HAS SHOWN US IN HIS PASSION

The whole sanctity and perfection of a soul consists in loving Jesus Christ, our God, our sovereign good, and our Redeemer. Whoever loves me, says Jesus Christ, shall be loved by my Eternal Father. "For the Father himself loves you because you have loved me" (Jn 16:27).

Some, says St. Francis de Sales, make perfection consist in an austere life; others in prayer; others in frequenting the Sacraments; others in alms-deeds. But they deceive themselves: perfection consists in loving God with our whole heart.

St. Paul wrote: "And over all these put on love, that is, the bond of perfection" (Col 3:14). It is charity which keeps united and preserves all the virtues that render a person perfect. Hence the famous phrase from St. Augustine, "Love God and do whatever you will." A soul which loves God is taught by that same love never to do anything that will displease him, and to leave nothing undone that may please him.

But perhaps God does not deserve all our love? "With age-old love I have loved you" (Jr 31:3). I was the first to love you, says the Lord. You were not yet in the world; indeed, the world itself was not, and already I loved you. As long as I am God, I loved you; as long as I have loved myself, I have also loved you.

With good reason, therefore, did St. Agnes, that young, holy virgin, reply to those who wished to unite her to an earthly spouse: "I am engaged to another lover. Depart, lovers of this world, cease to seek my love. My God was the first to love me. He has loved me from all eternity; it is but just then for me to give him all my affections and to love none other but him."

As Almighty God knew that we are won by kindness, he determined to lavish his gifts upon us and so take captive the affections of our hearts: "I drew them with human cords, with bands of love" (Ho 11:4). He set the snares by which we are caught, that is, the snares of love.

Such, exactly, are all the favors God gives us. After giving us a soul created in his own image, with memory, understanding and free will, and a body with its senses, he created heaven and earth out of love for us. He created the firmament, the stars, the planets, the seas, the rivers, the fountains, the hills, the plains, metals, fruits, a variety of animals — all his gifts to us that we might love him in gratitude for so many admirable gifts.

"Heaven and earth and all things tell me to love you," says St. Augustine. "My Lord, whatever I see on earth or above the earth, all speak to me and exhort me to love you. They all assure me that you made them out of love for me."

The Abbot de Rance, founder of La Trappe, when he stood outside his hermitage and surveyed the hills, the fountains, the birds, the flowers, the planets and the skies, felt himself animated by each of these creatures to love that God who had created all things through love.

In like manner, St. Mary Magdalene de Pazzi, when she held any beautiful flower in her hand, was enkindled by the sight of it with love for God. She would say, "And God, then, has thought from all eternity of creating this flower for love of me!" In that way that flower became, as it were, a dart of love which united her more and more to her God.

On the other hand, St. Teresa of Avila, at the sight of trees, fountains, rivers, lakes or meadows, declared that all these fair things upbraided her for her ingratitude in loving so coldly a God who created them that he might be loved by her.

But God was not satisfied with giving us so many beautiful creatures. He has gone to such lengths to gain our love as to give himself to us. The Eternal Father did not hesitate to give us even his only-begotten Son: "For God so loved the world that he gave his only Son" (Jn 3:16).

When the Eternal Father saw that we were all dead and deprived of his grace by sin, what did he do? For the great love he bore us, indeed as St. Paul says, for the immense love he bore us he sent his beloved Son to make atonement for us and to restore to us the life of which sin had robbed us: "God who is rich in mercy, because of the great love he had for us, even when we were dead in our transgressions, brought us to life with Christ" (Ep 2:4-5).

And in granting us his Son, not sparing his Son that he might spare us, he has granted us every other good together with him, his grace, his love and Paradise since these gifts are certainly much less than that of his Son: "He who did not spare his own Son but handed him over for us all, how will he not also give us everything else along with him?" (Rm 8:32).

And so also the Son, through his love for us, has given himself totally to us: "[He] has loved me and given himself up for me" (Gal 2:20). To redeem us from everlasting death and to recover for us divine grace and Heaven which we had forfeited, he became man and put on flesh like our own: "And the Word became flesh" (Jn 1:14).

Behold, then a God reduced to nothingness! "He emptied himself, taking the form of a slave, coming in human likeness and found human in appearance" (Ph 2:7). Behold, the sovereign of the world humbling himself so low as to assume the form of a servant and to subject himself to all the miseries which the rest of us endure.

What is more astonishing still is that he could very well have saved us without dying and without suffering at all. But no, he chose a life of sorrow and contempt, a death of bitterness and ignominy even to expiring on the cross, the gibbet of infamy, the award of the vilest criminals: "He humbled himself, becoming obedient to death, even death on a cross" (Ph 2:8).

But why, if he could have ransomed us without suffering, why should he choose to die, and to die on a cross? To show us how much he loved us: "Christ loved us and handed himself over for us as a sacrificial offering to God" (Ep 5:2). He loved us, and because he loved us, he delivered himself up to sorrows and ignominies and to a death more cruel than ever any man endured in this world.

That great lover of Jesus Christ, St. Paul, took occasion to say, "The love of Christ impels us . . ." (2 Cor 5:14). He wishes to show us by these words that it is not so much the sufferings themselves of Jesus Christ as his love in enduring them that impels us, indeed, obliges us to love him.

St. Francis de Sales comments on this passage in his *Treatise on the Love of God*: "When we remember that Jesus Christ, true God, has loved us to such an excess as to suffer death, death on the cross, for us our hearts are, as it were, put in a wine-press and suffer violence until love pours out of them, but a violence which the stronger it is the more delightful it becomes."

The love of Jesus for us created in him a longing desire for the moment of his death, when his love should be fully manifested to us. Therefore he said, "There is a baptism with which I must be baptized, and how great is my anguish until it is accomplished" (Lk 12:50). I have to be baptized in my own blood, and I long to accomplish that soon. Then people will know the love I bear them.

St. John writes of the night that Christ was to start his Passion: "Jesus knew that his hour had come to pass from this world to the Father. He loved his own in the world and he loved them to the end" (Jn 13:1). The Redeemer called that hour "his own hour" because the time of his death was the time he desired. He wanted to give the ultimate proof of his love for us.

But what could ever have induced a God to die as a criminal upon a cross between two felons with such an insult to his divine majesty? St. Bernard answers: "It was love, careless of its dignity!"

Love, indeed, when it tries to make itself known, does not seek what is becoming to the dignity of the lover but what will best serve to declare itself to the one loved. That is why St. Francis de Paola would exclaim, whenever he saw a crucifix, "O charity, O charity, O charity!" When we look at Jesus on the cross, we might well cry out, "O love, O love, O love!"

St. Lawrence Justinian could write, "We see Wisdom itself infatuated through the excess of love." Once, when in ecstasy, St. Mary Magdalene de Pazzi took up a wooden crucifix and cried out, "Yes, my Jesus, you are mad with love. I repeat it and will always say it: my Jesus you are mad with love!"

Oh, if we would only pause and, looking at Jesus on the cross, consider the love he has borne for each one of us!

But, in order to grow towards a more mature, a more perfect love of Christ, St. Thomas Aquinas suggests some means to that end in his discourse on the Love of God:

1. Constantly remember the benefits God has granted, both in general and in particular.
2. Consider the infinite goodness of God who is ever waiting to do us good and who always loves us and seeks love from us.
3. Avoid everything that could offend God.
4. Be detached from material goods, riches, honors and sensual pleasures.

No one can deny that, of all devotions, devotion to the Passion of Jesus Christ is the most useful, most tender and most agreeable to God, one that gives the greatest consolation to sinners and at the same time most powerfully enkindles loving hearts. It is through his Passion that Christ bestowed so many blessings on us.

From it we have hope of pardon, courage against temptations, confidence in salvation. From it we receive so many insights into truth, so many calls to love, so many promptings to improve our spiritual lives.

St. Bonaventure insists, "If you would make progress, meditate daily on the Passion of the Lord. Nothing works such an entire sanctification in the soul as meditating on the Passion of Christ." St. Augustine was of the opinion that one tear shed over the memory of the Passion was worth more than a to fast weekly on bread and water for a whole year. When someone suggested to St. Francis of Assisi that he read a certain pious work, he replied, "My book is Jesus crucified!"

(St. Alphonsus suggests that, at the end of each section, there be a period devoted to prayer, affections and a visit to Mary)

B. HOW MUCH JESUS DESERVES OUR LOVE AS HE HAS SHOWN IN INSTITUTING THE MOST HOLY SACRAMENT OF THE ALTAR.

"Jesus knew that his hour had come . . . He loved his own in the world and he loved them to the end" (Jn 13:1). Our most loving Savior, knowing that his hour was now come for leaving this earth, desired before he went to die for us, to leave us the greatest possible mark of his love — and this was the gift of the Most Holy Sacrament.

At death, people leave their most prized possessions to the ones they love most. But at his death what did Christ choose to leave? He gave us his own body, his own blood, his soul and divinity, indeed his whole self without reserve. He gave us all; he held nothing back.

The Council of Trent (Sess. 13, c.2) says that in this gift of the Eucharist Jesus Christ desired, as it were, to pour forth all the riches of the love that he had for humanity. St. Paul observes that Jesus desired to bestow this gift on us on the very night itself when they were planning his death: "The Lord Jesus, on the night he was handed over, took bread and, after he had given thanks, broke it and said, 'This is my body that is for you'" (1 Cor 11:23-24).

This Sacrament has been rightly named by St. Thomas Aquinas, "the Sacrament of love, the pledge of love."

Sacrament of love; for love was the only motive which induced

Jesus Christ to give us, in it, his whole self. Pledge of love; because if we ever doubted his love, here was the proof.

St. Bernard calls this Sacrament "the love of loves" because this gift comprehends all the other gifts bestowed upon us by our Lord — creation, redemption, predestination to glory; so that the Eucharist is not only a pledge of the love of Jesus Christ but of Paradise, which he also desires to give us.

The prophet Isaiah wanted the whole world to praise God for the wonderful ways in which he shows his love: "Give thanks to the Lord, acclaim his name; among the nations make known his deeds, proclaim how exalted is his name. Sing praise to the Lord for his glorious achievement" (Is 12:4-5).

But who could ever have thought — if he had not done it himself — that the Incarnate Word would conceal himself under the appearances of bread in order to become our food? "Does it not seem folly," says St. Augustine, "to say: 'Eat my flesh drink my blood?'" (*On Ps.* 33).

When Jesus Christ revealed to his disciples the Sacrament he desired to leave them, some of them could not bring themselves to believe him and they left, saying: "How can this man give us his flesh to eat? . . . This saying is hard; who can accept it?" (Jn 6:52, 60).

But that which one could neither conceive nor believe, the great love of Jesus Christ both thought of and accomplished. "Take and eat," he said to his disciples before he went out to die; and through them he said it to all of us.

Receive and eat: but what food shall that be, O Savior of the world, which you wanted to give us before you died? "Take and eat; this is my body." This is not earthly food; it is I myself who give myself entirely to you.

And how much he desires to come into our souls in Holy Communion! "I have eagerly desired to eat this Passover with you before I suffer" (Lk 22:15). So he spoke on that night in which he instituted this Sacrament of Love. "Eagerly have I desired" — the excessive love which he had for us caused to him to speak thus. These are the words of a most burning love.

To make it easy for all to receive him, he desired to leave himself under the appearance of bread. If he had chosen some rare or costly food, the poor would have been deprived of this, of him. No, Jesus would come under the form of bread which costs little and can be found everywhere so that he would be most accessible to all.

Not only does he invite us, exhort us, to receive Holy Communion, he also gave the precept, "Take and eat; this is my body." And further: "Unless you eat the flesh of the Son Man and drink his blood, you do not have life in you. Whoever eats my flesh and drinks my blood has eternal life and I will raise him up on the last day" (Jn 6:53-54).

Why does Jesus so desire to come to us in Holy Communion? Lovers desire that the two should be one. Love always longs to be united to the loved one. If this is so true of human love, how much more is it true of divine love?

So great is that love that it could not be satisfied even with the great gifts of his Incarnation and his Passion on the Cross. He desired a way in which he could give himself to each one of us entirely and intimately. This is the reason he instituted the Sacrament of the Altar: "Whoever eats my flesh and drinks my blood remains in me and I in him" (Jn 6:56).

In Holy Communion Jesus unites himself to the soul and the soul to Jesus, and not merely by affection; it is a real and true union. One cannot do or think of doing anything which gives greater pleasure to Jesus than to communicate frequently and with dispositions suitable to the great guest who is received.

Note I have said "suitable" not worthy. Who but God would be worthy to receive God? By "suitable," I mean such dispositions as become a created being, wounded by sin.

We must understand that there is nothing from which we can derive such profit as from Holy Communion. The Eternal Father has made Jesus Christ the possessor of all heavenly treasures: "The Father had put everything into his power" (Jn 13:3).

Therefore, when Jesus Christ comes into the soul in Holy Communion, he brings with him boundless treasures of grace.

Consequently after Holy Communion we can say with the wise man, "All good things together came to me" (Ws 7:11). No wonder the saints agree that the Sacrament of the Eucharist is far more powerful for the sanctification of souls than all other spiritual means of grace.

As the Council of Trent (Sess. 13, c. 2) teaches, Holy Communion is that great remedy which frees us from venial sin and helps preserve us against mortal sin. The acts of love we make when receiving Holy Communion obtain forgiveness from venial sins and increases in our souls the greater graces to help us avoid mortal sin.

This Sacrament, above all others, inflames our souls with divine love: "God is love" (1 Jn 4:8). He is also a fire which consumes all earthly affections in our hearts: "He is a consuming fire" (Dt 4:24). It was for this very purpose that the Son of God came to earth: "I have come to set the earth on fire, and how I wish it were already blazing!" (Lk 12:49).

What flames of love Jesus Christ lights up in the hearts of everyone who receives him devoutly in this Sacrament!

Someone, however, will say, "That's the very reason I do not communicate frequently, because I see that I am so cold in the love of God." Jean Gerson answers such a person by saying, "Do you willingly stay away from the fire when you are cold? Rather, because you feel yourself cold should you so much the more frequently approach this Sacrament if you really desire to love Jesus Christ."

St. Bonaventure wrote, "Although it be with lukewarmness, still approach, trusting the mercy of God. The more one feels sick, the greater the need for the physician."

St. Francis de Sales taught that there are two sorts of persons who should receive Holy Communion frequently: "the perfect in order to remain so, and the imperfect in order to become perfect." For frequent Communion it is highly useful to have a great desire to become a saint and to grow in the love of Jesus Christ.

(*Prayers, affections and a visit to Mary*)

C. THE GREAT CONFIDENCE WE OUGHT TO HAVE IN THE LOVE WHICH JESUS CHRIST HAS SHOWN US AND IN ALL HE HAS DONE FOR US.

David placed all his hope of salvation in his future Redeemer: "Into your hands I commend my spirit; you will redeem me, O Lord, O faithful God" (Ps 31:5). How much more ought we to say this prayer with confidence in Jesus Christ who has come and accomplished the work of redemption.

If we have great reason to fear everlasting death because of our sins, we have far greater reason to hope for everlasting life through the merits of Jesus Christ. These are infinitely more powerful for our salvation than our sins are for our damnation.

We have sinned and have deserved Hell; the Redeemer has come to take upon himself all of our offenses and to make satisfaction for them by His sufferings. "Yet it was our infirmities that he bore, our sufferings that he endured" (Is 53:4).

At the moment of grievous sin, the decree of eternal death is written, but what has our merciful Redeemer done? "Obliterating the bond against us, with its legal claims, which was opposed to us, he also removed it from our midst, nailing it to the Cross" (Col 2:14). He canceled by his blood the decree of our condemnation so that we may see on the Cross our hope of pardon and everlasting life.

How far more powerfully does the blood of Jesus speak for us. You have approached "Jesus, the mediator of a new covenant, and the sprinkled blood that speaks more eloquently than that of Abel" (Heb 12:24). It is as if St. Paul had said, "Your sins cry out against you but the blood of the Redeemer pleads in your favor. Divine justice cannot but be appeased by the voice of this precious blood."

It is true that we will have to render a rigorous account to the Eternal Judge for all our sins. But who is to be our Judge? "He has given all judgment to his Son" (Jn 5:22). Let us take comfort in the fact that the Eternal Father has committed our judgment to our own Redeemer. St. Paul encourages us by writing, "Who will condemn? It is Christ Jesus who died, rather was raised, who is also at the right hand of God, who indeed intercedes for us" (Rm 5:34).

St. Thomas of Villanova says, "What do you fear, O sinner, if you detest your sin? How will he condemn you, who died in order not to condemn you? How will he cast you from him if you return to his feet, he who came from Heaven to seek you at the very time you were flying from him?"

And if we fear that because of our human frailty we may fall to the constant attacks of the enemy, we have to take St. Paul's advice, "Persevere in running the race that lies before us while keeping our eyes fixed on Jesus, the leader and perfecter of faith. For the sake of the joy that lay before him he endured the cross, despising its shame, and has taken his place at the right of the throne of God" (Heb 12:1-2).

We can go out for spiritual battle with great courage, looking at Jesus crucified who from the Cross offers us his assistance, the victory and the crown. In the past we fell into sin because we stopped looking at the wounds and the pains endured by our Redeemer, and we did not ask him for help. For the future, keep sight of the love he proved by his suffering for us and take courage from the help he promises.

Oh, the two great mysteries of hope and love for us — the Passion of Jesus Christ and the Sacrament of the Altar — mysteries we couldn't even imagine if faith had not assured us of them. These two mysteries should consume our hearts with love!

"Let us confidently approach the throne of grace to receive mercy and to find grace for timely help" (Heb 4:16). The throne of grace is the Cross from which Jesus dispenses grace and mercy to all who come to him. The merits of Christ crucified have enriched us with all the divine treasures and has made us capable of every grace we can desire. "In him you were enriched in every way . . . so that you are not lacking in any spiritual grace" (1 Cor 1:5, 7).

The gift of redemption is greater than sin: "But the gift is not like the transgression. For if by that one transgression the many died, how much more did the grace of God and the gracious gift of the one man, Jesus Christ, overflow for the many" (Rm 5:15). Where sin has abounded, grace has superabounded!

Therefore we can hope for every favor and grace through the

merits of Christ: "Amen, amen, I say to you, whatever you ask the Father in my name he will give you" (Jn 16:23). How can the Father deny us when he himself has given his only-begotten Son? "He who did not spare his own Son but handed him over for us all, how will he not give us everything else along with him?" (Rm 8:32).

St. Paul says "everything" so that no grace is excepted, neither pardon, nor perseverance, nor holy love, nor perfection, nor Paradise. But we must pray to him. God is all liberality, "enriching all who call upon him" (Rm 10:12).

I will close this section by quoting from the letters of Venerable John of Avila:

> "Do not forget that Jesus Christ is the mediator between the Eternal Father and ourselves. We are beloved by him and united to him by such strong bonds of love that nothing can break them so long as one does not dissolve them by a mortal sin.
>
> "The blood of Jesus cries out and asks mercy for us. The death of Jesus has put to death our sins. Those who are lost are not lost for want of the means of satisfaction but because they would not avail themselves of the sacraments, the means of profiting by the satisfaction made by Christ.
>
> "Jesus said to his Father: 'Father, they are your gift to me. I wish that where I am they also may be with me' (Jn 17:24). Love has conquered hatred so we have been pardoned and loved and are secure of never being abandoned, so strong is the tie that binds us.
>
> "The Lord told us through Isaiah, 'Can a mother forget her infant, be without tenderness for the child of her womb? Even should she forget, I will never forget you' (Is 49:15-16). He has graven us in his hands with his own blood. We should not trouble ourselves about anything since everything is ordained by those hands which were nailed to the Cross in testimony of the love he has for us.

"Nothing can so trouble us on which Jesus Christ cannot reassure us. Let the sins I have committed surround me, let the devil lay snares for me, let fears for the future accuse me — by demanding mercy from the most tender Jesus Christ, who has loved me even until death I cannot possibly lose confidence. I see myself so highly valued that God gave himself for me.

"Jesus, you are the sure haven of those in peril. O most watchful Pastor, he deceives himself who does not put his trust in you, if only he has the will to amend his life."

If you believe that the Eternal Father has given you his Son, believe also that he will give you everything else which is infinitely less than his Son. Do not think that Jesus Christ is forgetful of you since he has left you as the greatest memorial and pledge of his love, himself in the Most Holy Sacrament of the Altar.

(Affections, prayers and visit to Mary)

D. HOW MUCH ARE WE OBLIGED TO LOVE JESUS CHRIST?

Jesus Christ, as God, has a claim on all of our love, but by the love which he has shown for us he wished to put us, so to speak, under the necessity of loving him, at least in gratitude for all that he has done and suffered for us. He has greatly loved us that we might love him greatly.

"Why does God love us," ask St. Bernard, "but that he may be loved?" And Moses said the same thing centuries earlier, "And now Israel, what does the Lord, your God, ask of you but to fear the Lord, your God, and follow his ways exactly, to love and serve the Lord, your God, with all your heart and all your soul" (Dt 10:12).

St. Paul goes further, "Love is the fulfillment of the law" (Rm 13:10). For "fulfilling" the Greek text has "embracing." Love embraces the entire law.

Who, indeed, at the sight of a crucified God dying for our love can refuse to love him? Those thorns, those nails, that cross, those wounds and that blood call upon us and irresistibly urge us to love him who has loved us so much. "He indeed died for all, so that those who live might no longer live for themselves but for him who for their sake died" (2 Cor 5:15).

Jesus desires that we continually remember his Passion and it saddens him when we forget it. Suppose a person endured trials, blows and imprisonment for a friend who later never gave it a thought or would even mention it. On the contrary, how gratifying it would be if the friend constantly spoke of it with real gratitude.

So it pleases the Lord when we preserve the memory of his Passion with a loving and grateful recollection of it. Jesus was the desire of the ancient patriarchs, the desire of the nations and how much more should his Passion and death make us desire to respond with love to his proof of love?

This is the reason why he instituted the Sacrament of the Holy Eucharist on the day before his death, and gave us the command that as often as we should be nourished with his most sacred flesh we should be mindful of his death.

"For I received from the Lord what I have also handed on to you, that the Lord Jesus, on the night he was handed over, took bread, and, after he had given thanks, broke it and said 'This is my body that is for you. Do this in remembrance of me.'

"In the same way also the cup, after supper, saying 'This cup is the new covenant in my blood. Do this as often as you drink it, in remembrance of me.' For as often as you eat this bread and drink this cup, you proclaim the death of the Lord until he comes" (1 Cor 11:23-26).

Therefore how pleasing it must be to Jesus Christ when we think of his Passion frequently. It was for this reason that he left the great Sacrament of the Altar that we might keep in mind continually, with grateful recall, all that he did for love of us. This will increase our love of him. Well does St. Francis de Sales call Mount Calvary "a mountain of lovers." It is impossible to remember that mount and not love Jesus Christ who died there for love of us.

St. Thomas of Villanova says that we cannot look at the Cross without seeing the proof of Christ's love for us. St. Bernard adds, "the Cross and every wound of our Blessed Redeemer cry aloud to make us understand the love he bears for us." All the words and works of the Incarnate Word invite our loving response, but the Cross is the ultimate proof of his love for us and the need for our reply in kind.

"Love is a great thing," writes St. Bernard in his treatise on the Song of Songs. Solomon, speaking of divine wisdom, which is holy charity, calls it an infinite treasure. "For to men she is an unfailing treasure; those who gain this treasure win the friendship of God" (Ws 7:14).

St. Thomas Aquinas says that charity is not only the queen of virtues but that, wherever she reigns she draws along with her all the other virtues and directs them all to uniting us to a closer union with God. St. Bernard says, "Charity is a virtue uniting us with God."

Scripture testifies to this over and over again: "Those who love me I also love" (Pr 8:17); "Whoever loves me will keep my word and my Father will love him and we will come to him and make our dwelling with him" (Jn 14:23); "God is love, and whoever remains in love remains in God and God in him" (1 Jn 4:16).

St. Augustine comments that "nothing is so hard that it cannot be subdued by the fire of love." And in another place he writes, "In that which is loved, either there is no labor, or the labor is loved." St. Francis de Sales adds that they delude themselves "who place virtue in anything else than in loving God."

It is not necessary to be rich in this world, to gain the esteem of others, to lead a life of ease, to enjoy dignities, to have a reputation for learning; it is only necessary to love God and to do his will. For this purpose he created us, guards us, and leads us to Paradise.

To acquire a true love of Jesus Christ should be our only care. The masters of the spiritual life describe the marks of true love:

1. *fearful* — dreading the possibility of displeasing God;
2. *generous* — doing all for the glory of God, no matter how difficult;

3. *strong* — defeating temptations and desolation;
4. *obedient* — seeking the divine will in everything;
5. *pure* — loving God alone because that is what he deserves;
6. *ardent* — seeking to share this divine love with everyone;
7. *inebriating* — going out of one's self as if nothing existed but the love of God;
8. *unitive* — striving to unite one's human will to the will of God; and
9. *longing* — yearning for Heaven.

But no one speaks so eloquently of love as St. Paul: "If I have all faith so as to move mountains but do not have love, I am nothing. If I give away everything I own, and if I hand over my body to be burned but do not have love, I gain nothing" (1 Cor 13:2-3). The moving of mountains, the working of miracles, even martyrdom, have no profit in them if they lack charity, love.

Then Paul goes on to give the mark of love and the virtues that attend charity: "Love is patient, love is kind. It is not jealous nor pompous, it is not inflated, it is not rude, it does not seek its own interests, it is not quick-tempered, it does not brood over injury, it does not rejoice over wrongdoing but rejoices with the truth. It bears all things, believes all things, hopes all things, endures all things" (1 Cor 13:4-7).

We shall now proceed to consider these holy practices to see if the love we owe to Jesus Christ really reigns in our souls and what virtues we must pursue to persevere and advance in this holy love.

(Affections, prayers, visit to Mary)

I.

Charity is patient (1 Cor 13:4 — Patience)

Those who love Jesus are long-suffering.

This earth is a place for meriting and therefore it is a place for suffering. Our true country, where God has prepared repose for us in everlasting joy, is Paradise. We have but a short time to spend in this world so much must be accomplished in this short time.

"Man born of woman is short-lived and full of troubles" (Job 14:1). We must suffer; all must suffer. The just and the unjust must each carry his own cross. Carry it with patience to be saved; carry it with impatience and be lost. The test of suffering defines the difference between the wheat and the chaff.

Those who humble themselves under tribulations and are resigned to the will of God are wheat for Paradise. Those who grow haughty and are enraged estrange themselves from God and become the chaff.

When the day of our judgment arrives, we must be found conformed to Christ. "For those he foreknew he also predestined to be conformed to the image of his Son" (Rm 8:29). This is the reason the Eternal Word came to earth — to teach us by his example, to carry with patience the cross which God sends us: "For to this you have been called, because Christ also suffered for you, leaving you an example that you should follow in his footsteps" (1 P 2:21).

Think of the poverty Christ endured, the pain and the humiliation of the Passion! As Isaiah foretold, "He was spurned and avoided by men, a man of suffering, accustomed to infirmity, one of those from whom men hide their faces, spurned and we held him in no esteem" (Is 53:3).

If God so subjected his beloved Son to such suffering, he expects suffering to strengthen us. "For whom the Lord loves he disciplines; he scourges every son he acknowledges" (Heb 12:6). For this reason

St. Teresa said that she would not exchange all of her trials and troubles for all the treasures of the world. After her death she privately revealed that her immense reward in heaven was not because of all her good works, but for the sufferings she cheerfully endured.

The person who loves God in suffering earns a double reward in Paradise. St. Vincent de Paul said it was a great misfortune to be free from suffering in this life. St. Francis of Assisi felt that a day without a cross was a day when God avoided him. St. John Chrysostom said that a soul to whom God gave the grace of suffering had a greater grace than that of raising the dead. He felt that St. Paul received a greater grace from suffering chains for Christ than from being raised to the third heaven in ecstasy.

"And let perseverance be perfect so that you may be perfect and complete, lacking in nothing" (Jm 1:4). Suffering with patient perseverance the crosses God sends makes the soul more Christlike.

St. John saw all the saints clothed in white with palms in their hands (Rv 7:9). The palm is the symbol of martyrdom, yet not all the saints were martyrs. St. Gregory the Great replies that all the saints were martyrs of the sword or of patience. He states that "we can be martyrs without the sword if we keep patience."

St. Teresa pointed out that "God never sends a trial without the grace to rewarding it with some favor." For motivation, she says, look at the wounds of Christ; our trials will never reach that far! St. Paul taught his too: "I consider that the sufferings of this present time are as nothing compared with the glory to be revealed in us" (Rm 8:18).

With what readiness, then, should we embrace our crosses when we know that the sufferings of this transitory life will gain for us everlasting beatitude. "For this momentary light affliction is producing for us an eternal weight of glory beyond all comparison" (2 Cor 4:16).

Whoever desires the crown of Paradise must undergo combat and suffer: "If we persevere with him we shall also reign with him" (2 Tm 2:14). We cannot get a reward without merit, and no merit is to be had without patience. The person who strives with the greatest patience should have the greatest reward.

When the temporal goods of this world are in question, the

worldly strive to get as much as they can, but when it is a question of eternal goods they say, "It's enough to get just a little corner in Heaven."

Such is not the language of the saints. Detached, they are satisfied with anything in this world; even more, they strip themselves of all earthly goods. But concerning eternal goods, they strive to obtain them in as large a measure as possible. Which is the wiser and more prudent way?

But even with this present life, those who practice the most patience have the most peace of mind. Let us be convinced that in this valley of tears true peace of heart cannot be found except by those who lovingly embrace their crosses to please Almighty God. "If anyone wishes to come after me," says the Lord, "he must deny himself and take up his cross daily and follow me" (Lk 9:23). This must be done, not by constraint and against our will, but with humility, patience and love.

St. Catherine of Genoa has some wise words to add to this thought: "To attain union with God, adversities are indispensable. By them God aims at destroying all our corrupt propensities both within and without. All injuries, contempt, abandonment by loved ones, temptations and mortification are necessary in the highest degree so that we may carry on the fight until, by repeated victories, we come to extinguish all viciousness within us."

"The patient man is better than the valiant" (Pr 16:32). God is pleased with a person who practices mortification by fasting, haircloths, and discipline because they show courage. But he is even more pleased with those who have the fortitude to bear patiently the crosses that he sends. St. Francis de Sales said that it is always better to leave the choice of purification in the hands of God, rather than in our own.

(*Affections, prayers and visit to Mary*)

II.

Charity is kind
(1 Cor. 13:4 — Meekness, Gentleness)

He who loves Jesus loves meekness.

St. Francis de Sales wrote: "Humble meekness is the virtue of virtues." Thus one who loves God loves all whom God loves, eagerly seeking every occasion to assist all, console all, and help people to be happy.

This gentleness should be shown especially to the poor who are so often harshly treated by others, and to the sick who are suffering under infirmities that so often receive little attention when needed. It is especially effective in dealing with enemies: "Conquer evil with good" (Rm 12:21).

"There is nothing," wrote St. Francis de Sales," that gives so much edification to our neighbor than kindness of behavior." St. Vincent de Paul declared of Francis that he had never met a kinder man in his life. This kindness or gentleness, meekness if you will, helps form a true likeness of Jesus in us.

This is especially true of superiors who have to lead others. It is much better to direct by request than by command. St. Jane Frances de Chantal, the foundress of the Visitation Order, wrote: "I have tried various methods of governing but I have not found any better than that of meekness and forbearance.

Even more, a superior should be kind even in the correction of faults. It is one thing to correct with firmness and quite another with harshness. It is necessary at times to correct with firmness, when the fault is serious and especially if it has been repeated, but be on guard against harsh and angry correction. Correction with anger does more harm than good. In his epistle, James warns about this (Jm 3:13-18).

If a harsh word is needed to get the attention of the offender, the correction should be finished with gentleness. If the person is agitated or upset, it is better to defer the correction until the anger has

abated, or otherwise the indignation and frustration may be com-
pounded.

When Jesus and his followers were refused hospitality in a
Samaritan town, James and John wanted to call down fire from
heaven, but Jesus rebuked them (Lk 9:55). The Son of Man came on
earth to save souls, not to destroy. He personally gave them the
example of one who was meek and humble of heart.

With what gentleness he treated the woman taken in the act of
adultery: "Woman, where are they? Has no one condemned you?
Neither do I condemn you" (Jn 8:10-11). He only required that she
go and sin no more.

The same gentleness is shown in the way Jesus treated the
Samaritan woman (Jn 4), and his meekness abounds in miracle after
miracle, parable after parable. He treated Judas with sweet reason:
"Do you betray the Son of Man with a kiss?" (Lk 22:48). He converted
St. Peter after the denial just by looking at him (Lk 22:61).

St. Bernard remarks that some people are gentle as long as
things go their way, but at the slightest opposition they erupt like Mt.
Vesuvius. The person who loves God maintains an imperturbable
peace of heart, and shows it in action and countenance both in
prosperity and adversity.

Adversity brings out a person's real character. St. Francis de
Sales dearly loved the Order of the Visitation, which cost him so much
labor. He saw it several times in imminent danger of dissolution, but
he never for a moment lost his peace of mind. He was ready, if such
was the will of God, to see it entirely destroyed.

Whenever we have to reply to an insult, be careful to answer
with meekness. "A mild answer calms wrath" (Pr 15:1). A mild reply
usually is enough to quench the spark of anger. In case we feel
irritated, it is best to keep silence. Otherwise we will pour out all sorts
of words that afterwards prove faulty.

And when it happens that we ourselves commit some fault, we
must practice meekness in our own regard. To be exasperated at
ourselves after a fault is not humility, but a subtle pride as if we were

anything else than weak and miserable. St. Teresa comments, "The humility that disturbs does not come from God."

To be angry with ourselves after the commission of a fault is a fault worse than the one committed and will be the occasion of many other faults. A soul that lets itself get troubled in this way knows little of God and of what God requires. Whenever we commit a fault, we should turn to God with humility, confidence in him, and the craving of his forgiveness.

Pray, rather, with words like these of St. Catherine of Genoa, "O Lord, this is the produce of my own garden. I love you with my whole heart and I repent of any displeasure I have given you. Grant me your assistance so that I will never do the like again."

(Affections, prayers, and visit to Mary)

III.

Charity does not envy (1 Cor 13:4 — Envy)

The soul that loves Jesus does not envy the great ones of this world, but only those who are greater lovers of Jesus Christ.

In his work on Christian morals, St. Gregory the Great explains this next characteristic of charity in saying that as charity despises all earthly greatness, it cannot possibly be provoked to envy by such greatness.

But we must distinguish between two kinds of envy, one evil and the other holy. The evil kind is that which envies the worldly goods possessed by others. Holy envy, far from wanting to be like the great ones of the world, has compassion for those who live in the midst of honors and material pleasures.

The charitable soul seeks and desires God alone and has no other aim besides that of loving God as much as possible. There is a pious envy of those who love God more, since the truly charitable person would, if possible, surpass the very seraphim in loving him.

Those whose primary aim is the love of God delight the heart of God and cause him to say, "You have ravished my heart, my sister, my bride; you have ravished my heart with one glance of your eyes" (Sg 4:9). That one glance is the desire to love God above all things.

Worldly people look at things with many glances, many reasons. They do things to gain honor, wealth, position, and pleasure. The saints have that one single glance, that one aim, directing themselves towards God. "Whom have I in heaven? And when I am not with you, the earth delights me not . . . God is the rock of my heart and my portion forever" (Ps 73:25-26). St. Paulinus exclaimed, "Let the rich enjoy their riches and the kings their kingdoms. You, O Christ, are my treasure and my kingdom."

It is not enough to perform good works, but they must be done well. As was said of Christ, "He does all things well" (Mk 7:37). Many actions may in themselves be praiseworthy, but from being performed for some other purpose than for the glory of God, they are often of little or no value in his sight. Some, even in such holy works as preaching, giving missions, hearing confessions and the like, do it for honor, prestige or self-interest.

O this accursed self-love that causes us to lose all or part of the fruit of our good actions! Purity of intention, doing good works for the love of God, is immensely important if these works are to be pleasing to God.

Our Lord said, "Take care not to perform righteous deeds in order that people may see them; otherwise you will have no recompense from your heavenly Father" (Mt 6:1). Whoever works for his own gratification has already received his wages. "Amen, I say to you, they have received their reward" (Mt 6:5). It is a reward that vanishes as quickly as smoke.

The Prophet Haggai says that whoever labors for anything else than to please God puts his reward in a sack full of holes, which, when he comes to open it, he will find entirely empty: "And he who earned wages earned them for a bag with holes in it" (Hg 1:6).

People like that are deeply troubled when some good work does not succeed as they had projected. This is a sign that they didn't have the glory of God as the principal reason for their activity. Whoever undertakes something solely for the glory of God is not troubled at all if it is not successful. In truth, by working with a pure intention he has already gained his object, which was to please God.

Here are the signs that we are working solely for God in any spiritual undertaking:

1. If we are not disturbed by the failure of our plans because when we see it is not the will of God, neither is it ours;
2. If we rejoice at the good done by others as heartily as if we ourselves had done it;
3. If we have no preference for one position over another but willingly accept whatever position is given us;
4. If after our actions we do not seek thanks or approval, or if the work fails, we are not upset with being faulted; and
5. If the world does applaud us, we are not unduly elated.

This is to enter into the joy of the Lord; that is, to enjoy the enjoyment of God as is promised to his faithful servants. "Well done, my good and faithful servant . . . Come share your master's joy" (Mt 25:21). And if it falls to our lot to do something pleasing to God, what more can we desire?

Purity of intention is called the heavenly alchemy by which iron is turned into gold; that is to say, the most trivial and ordinary actions when done for God become the gold of holy love.

Those who have nothing else in view in their undertakings than the divine will, enjoy that holy liberty of spirit which belongs to the children of God. This enables them to embrace everything that pleases Jesus Christ, be it sweet or bitter. With the same feelings of peace they address themselves to small and great works, to the pleasant and the unpleasant; it is enough for them if they please God.

Many, on the other hand, are willing to serve God as long as they can set the conditions pleasing to themselves. They will do this work in this place at this time, etc. Such persons do not have freedom of the spirit but are slaves of self-love. They lead a troubled life because the yoke of Christ has become a burden to them.

The true lovers of Jesus Christ care only to do what pleases him, for the reason that it pleases him, when he wills and where he wills. This is what is meant by loving Jesus Christ with a pure love. We must make every effort to grow in this fashion, battling our self-love and inclination to seek important and honorable functions, and such as suit our inclinations. We must be detached from all exercises, even spiritual ones, when the Lord wishes us to be occupied in other ways.

(Affections, prayers, and visit to Mary)

IV.

Charity is not pompous
(1 Cor 13:4 — Lukewarmness)

*He who loves Jesus Christ avoids lukewarmness
and seeks perfection.*

According to St. Gregory the Great, "charity is not pompous" expresses the concept that the charitable person has so given himself up more and more to the love of God that whatever is not right and holy is ignored. St. Paul teaches the same thing when he writes, "And over all these put on love, that is, the bond of perfection" (Col 3:14). And, since charity delights in perfection, it abhors the lukewarmness with which some persons serve God, putting at risk the loss of charity itself.

A. LUKEWARMNESS

It must be observed that there are two kinds of lukewarmness or tepidity: one avoidable, the other unavoidable.

1. Unavoidable Lukewarmness

From the lukewarmness that is unavoidable, even the saints themselves were not exempt. This involves all the failings that are committed by us without full consent but spring merely from our human frailty. Such are, for example, distraction at prayer, interior anxiety, useless words, vain curiosity, the wish to be accepted, tastes in eating and drinking, the movements of concupiscence not quickly repressed, and such like.

We ought to avoid these defects as much as possible, but owing to the weakness of our nature, caused by the infection of sin, it is impossible to avoid them altogether. We ought to avoid them as something less pleasing to God when we become aware of them, but we should beware of making them a subject of alarm or anxiety. Dismiss them from mind, and make no account of them.

St. Francis de Sales taught that since they come involuntarily, so they are canceled involuntarily. An act of sorrow, an act of love cancels them. The Council of Trent taught that Holy Communion is "an antidote by which we are freed from daily faults." These faults do not hinder our pursuit of perfection.

2. Avoidable Lukewarmness

The lukewarmness that does hinder perfection is that tepidity which is avoidable when a person commits deliberate venial faults. With the help of divine graces these can be avoided. St. Teresa prayed, in her *Way of Perfection*, "May God deliver you from deliberate sin, small as it may be." Such, for example, are willful untruths, little detractions, cursing, derision of one's neighbor, animosities and inordinate attachments.

St. Teresa called them "a little worm" which can eat into the other virtues. She adds, "By means of small things the devil goes about making holes for great things to enter." Such deliberate faults close us off from the greater graces and spiritual insights. They can make us weary of spiritual exercises and perhaps leave them out.

This is the meaning of this warning: "I know your works; I know that you are neither cold nor hot. I wish you were either hot or cold. But, because you are lukewarm, neither hot nor cold, I will spit you out of my mouth" (Rv 3:15-16).

What a thought! Better to be cold — to be deprived of the life of sanctifying grace? Yes, in a certain sense, because then the voice of conscience has something to reproach and urge on the sinner to repentance. The tepid person slumbers in his faults and even feels at ease with them and so has no need, it seems to him, to correct them. He has made a truce with them. He makes the cure, as it were, desperate.

B. REMEDIES AGAINST LUKEWARMNESS

The means to cast off tepidity and to pursue perfection are five in number:

1. The Desire for Perfection;
2. The Resolution to Attain It;
3. Meditation or Mental Prayer;
4. Frequent Holy Communion; and
5. Prayer.

Let us consider each step:

1. Desire for Perfection

The first means, then, is the desire for perfection. Pious desires are the wings which lift us up from the earth. They give us the strength to walk towards perfection, and lighten the fatigue of the journey. One with the real desire for perfection continues to advance until that state is reached.

On the contrary, one who does not desire perfection will keep slipping backwards until he becomes more imperfect than before. St. Augustine says that "not to go forward in the way of God is to go backward." He who makes no effort to advance will find himself carried backward by the current of his fallen nature.

Some object: God doesn't want us all to be saints. That is a great mistake, for St. Paul tells us: "This is the will of God, your sanctification" (1 Th 4:3). God wishes us all to be saints, each according to his state in life, the priest as priest, the married as married, the businessman as businessman, the soldier as soldier, and so in every state in life.

As St. Teresa writes in her autobiography, "Let us enlarge our hearts from which we will derive immense good." She goes on, "We must beware of having poor desires, but rather put our confidence in God so that, by forcing ourselves continually onwards, we may, by degrees, arrive where by divine grace so many saints have arrived."

She cites her own experience with courageous souls who have made great progress in short periods of time. Then she adds, "God does not fail to repay every good desire even in this life for he is the friend of generous souls, provided only that they do not trust in themselves. God does not confer extraordinary favors except where his love has been earnestly sought after."

"We know," St. Paul teaches, "that all things work for good for those who love God" (Rm 8:28). Even past sins can contribute to our sanctification inasmuch as the recollection of them keeps us more humble, and more grateful when we witness the favors which God now lavishes on us. With his help, certainly not on our own, "I have the strength for everything through him who empowers me" (Ph 4:13).

2. Resolution

The second means of perfection is the resolution to belong wholly to God. Many are called to perfection, urged toward it by grace. They conceive a desire for it, but never really resolve to acquire it. The desire for perfection is not enough if it is not followed up by a strong resolve to attain it.

How many souls feed themselves on desires alone, without doing anything to follow up with suitable means. They say, "If only I could get away to a monastery," or "If only I had a different spouse," etc. Such desires do more harm than good. They become an excuse for inaction.

We must therefore desire perfection and resolutely take the means towards it. St. Teresa said, "God looks for us to begin with a resolve and then he will do the rest. The devil has no fear of irresolute souls."

Mental prayer must be used in order to take the means to acquire perfection. Some say many prayers but never come to a practical conclusion. Better a short prayer that produces fruit than all sorts of long, involved prayers.

But first we must have the strong resolution to pursue perfection and avoid all deliberate sins. True, by ourselves we cannot succeed, but this paves the way for the entrance of grace into our souls to strengthen this resolve. St. Francis de Sales advises, "Let us put ourselves into a state of pure and irrevocable abandonment of our entire being into God's hands, and in the firm resolution of never consenting to any sin, great or small."

This is what it means to have a delicate conscience, a necessary prelude to holiness. Note, it is not a scrupulous conscience. To be scrupulous is a defect and does harm. On this account it is necessary to obey our spiritual directors and rise above scruples. Scruples are nothing but vain and unreasonable alarms.

It is necessary to resolve on choosing the best, not only what is agreeable to God, but what is most agreeable to him without any reserve. St. Francis de Sales advises, "We must have a strong and constant reserve, giving ourselves totally to God without holding back anything. We must renew this resolution often. Then, as we advance towards perfection, the attraction itself grows in us. Finally, one will continually work for it without wearying."

We must begin at once since in the next life there is no more time to work, nor free will to merit, nor prudence to do well, nor wisdom or experience to take good counsel by, for after death what is done is done.

St. Charles Borromeo said, "Today I begin to serve God." And we should act in such a way as if we had done nothing good before today. Each day resolve to begin afresh to belong wholly to God. Don't try to compare yourself to others for, as St. Bernard remarked, "One cannot be perfect without being singular." We must overcome all, renounce all, in order to gain all.

O God, how little is our "all" that is given to Jesus Christ who has given his blood and his life for us. "He indeed died for all, so that those who live might no longer live for themselves but for him who for their sake died and was raised" (2 Cor 5:15).

3. Meditation or Mental Prayer

The third way of becoming a saint is mental prayer.

Jean Gerson had this to say: "He who does not meditate on the eternal truths cannot, without a miracle, lead the life of a Christian. The reason is that without mental prayer light fails us and we walk in the dark. The truths of faith are not seen by the eyes of the body but by the eyes of the mind when we meditate. He who fails to meditate on them fails to see them and therefore walks in the dark. Being in the dark, he easily grows attached to material things for the sake of which he loses sight of the eternal."

St. Teresa observed that "although we seem to discover in ourselves no imperfections, when God opens the eyes of the soul, usually through mental prayer, we see ourselves much more clearly." "Mental prayer," adds St. Bernard, "regulates the affections, directs the actions, keeps the affections of the soul in order, and directs all our actions to God."

Without mental prayer the affections become attached to the earth, the actions conform to the affections, and all sorts of disorder arises. Whoever leaves out mental prayer will soon leave off loving Jesus Christ. Prayer is the blessed furnace in which the fire of holy love is enkindled and kept alive. St. Teresa observed, "Whoever perseveres in the way of prayer always arrives, sooner or later."

In prayer we conceive holy thoughts, we practice devout affections, we excite great desires and form efficacious resolutions to give ourselves wholly to God. St. Aloysius Gonzaga remarked, "There will never be much perfection without much prayer."

We should not go to prayer expecting consolations, but we should pray solely to please God, to learn his will and to beg him for help. Prayer unattended with sensible consolations actually confers greater fruit.

One of the results of prayer is that we think constantly of God. "The true lover," says St. Teresa, "is ever mindful of the beloved." Prayer also makes us take pleasure in solitude where we can be alone with God but it also helps us keep an interior recollection while we go about the necessary tasks of our state in life.

The greatest danger is that without mental prayer we do not pray at all. I have written often about prayer, but there are a few things I want to say here. As the Bishop of Osma said, "Without prayer there is no communication with God for the preservation of virtue." How else can we be convinced of the means necessary for salvation, the ways to avoid temptation, and what to ask from God? Whosoever does not know the necessity of prayer will soon abandon it and put his soul in danger.

The subject of meditation? What greater than the Four Last Things — Death, Judgment, Hell and Heaven. Imagine yourself expiring on your deathbed, crucifix held firmly in hand and being about to enter eternity. Gaze on Christ dying for us. We must be moved by the sight of God so willing to seal his love for us with his blood! No wonder St. Francis de Sales called the Mount of Calvary the "mount of lovers."

4. Frequent Communion

The fourth means of perfection, and even of perseverance in the grace of God, is to receive Holy Communion frequently. A soul can do nothing more pleasing to Jesus Christ than to receive him often in the Sacrament of the Altar.

St. Teresa asserts that "there is no faster road to perfection than frequent Holy Communion." St. Bernard tells us that Holy Communion represses the movement of anger and incontinence. St. John Chrysostom says that Holy Communion pours into our souls a great inclination to virtue and a promptness to practice it, as well as the peace of soul that makes it warm and inviting.

The Council of Trent taught that Holy Communion delivers us from daily faults and preserves us from mortal ones.

A suitable preparation for mental prayer and a fervent thanksgiving afterwards will assure more abundant fruit from this great Sacrament. The communicant must, of course, be in the state of grace and should be moving away from deliberate venial sins in his daily life.

St. Teresa says: "After Communion let us be careful not to lose so good an opportunity of negotiating with God. His divine majesty is not accustomed to pay badly for his lodging, if he meets with a good reception."

Some protest weakly, "Oh, I am not worthy to receive Holy Communion often." Don't they realize that the more they refrain from Holy Communion the less worthy they become? The best way to become more worthy is to receive often. The person who considered himself worthy of so great a gift suffers from great pride.

Others excuse themselves by saying, "But in the past I was very bad." Don't they realize that it is the weakest who most need the physician and the medicine? Where else will they find so sure a cure?

Then there are those who say, "But I don't feel anything when I receive." Sensible devotions, "feelings," are not necessary. God does not always grant sensible devotion even to his most beloved souls. It is enough to have the devotion of a will determined to belong wholly to God and to make progress in divine love.

Why do some fear to receive Holy Communion? Well, of course, those in mortal sin must first repent. Some, while trying to live a good Christian life, are so embroiled in the things of this world that their spiritual life suffers. Others love God and would like to receive often, but because of prejudices or blind fear they do not approach the Holy Table. Oh timid, fearful souls, why not despise these fears and prejudices, and give heed to the voice of the Church?

Fervor can be kept alive in the soul by often making a spiritual Communion. As St. Thomas says, this consists in an ardent desire to receive Jesus in the Holy Sacrament.

This is how it might be phrased: "My Jesus, I believe that You are really present in the Most Holy Sacrament. I love You; I desire You; come into my soul. Never let me be separated from You."

A shorter version might be: "My Jesus, come to me. I long for You; I desire You. Let us remain ever united together." This spiritual Communion can be practiced several times a day, and whenever we are at prayer.

5. Prayer

The fifth and most necessary means for spiritual life and for obtaining the love of Jesus Christ is prayer.

In the first place, I say that by this means God convinces us of the great love he bears for us. What greater proof of affection can a person give than to say to him, "My friend, ask anything you want from me and I will give it to you"? But this is precisely what Our Lord says to us, "Ask and it will be given to you; seek and you will find; knock and it will be opened to you" (Mt 7:7). Therefore, prayer is called all-powerful with God to obtain every blessing.

The words of King David are very reassuring: "Blessed be God who refused me not my prayer or his kindness" (Ps 66:20). St. Augustine comments on this by writing, "As long as you see yourself persevering in prayer, the divine mercy will not fail you either."

What sympathy can there be for a beggar who, having a very rich master, and one who wants to help in anything if only he is asked, nevertheless still chooses to live in poverty rather than asking? Yet, St. Paul reminds us that our God is ready to "enrich all who call upon him" (Rm 10:12).

Humble prayer, then, obtains all from God. It is both useful and necessary for our salvation. This is especially true when praying for the gift of final perseverance, of dying in the grace of God, which is the grace absolutely necessary for our salvation and without which we would be lost forever.

The theologians tell us that prayer is a matter of necessity, since it is so clearly commanded by God (precept) but also because it is the ordinary means God expects us to use to obtain the graces we need (means).

Jesus "told them a parable about the necessity for them to pray always without becoming weary" (Lk 18:1). St. Paul understood this when he wrote, "Pray without ceasing" (1 Th 5:17). While we cannot merit the grace of final perseverance, prayer opens the way for it.

The Desert Fathers taught us the importance of frequent prayers of aspiration: " My Jesus, mercy!" "Come to my aid, O God of mercy!" "Turn to me; make haste to help me!" These and similar prayers were often on their lips.

Christ invites us with the words, "Until now you have not asked anything in my name; ask and you shall receive, so that your joy may be complete" (Jn 16:24). St. Augustine comments, "By promising he makes himself our debtor." And we can, indeed, ask with confidence, for Jesus told us, "Therefore I tell you, all that you ask for in prayer, believe that you will receive it and it shall be yours" (Mk 11:24).

Some may say, "I am a sinner and do not deserve to be heard." But Jesus Christ says, "Everyone who asks receives" (Lk 11:10) — everyone, both the just and the sinner. St. Thomas Aquinas teaches that the efficacy of prayer to obtain graces does not depend on our own merits but on the mercy of God who has promised to hear everyone who prays to him (*Summa Theologiae* 2.2, q. 178, a. 2). Our Redeemer, in order to remove from us all fear when we pray, said, "Amen, amen, I say to you, whatever you ask the Father in my name he will give to you" (Jn 16:23).

It is as if he invites sinners to ask for all the graces they want and need, and assures that they will be granted because of his love and merit. Note well he says to ask "in my name," that is to say "in the name of the Savior." These graces promised are what we need for eternal salvation. They do not refer to temporal favors which are only granted when they are profitable to eternal salvation. Do not hesitate to ask for temporal favors, but always on the condition that they will benefit our souls.

And while you pray to God, do not forget to recommend yourself at the same time to Mary, the dispenser of God's graces. It is Almighty God who bestows graces, but he bestows them through the hands of Mary. St. Bernard reminds us, "Let us seek grace and let us seek it through Mary, because what she seeks she finds and cannot be refused." If Mary prays for us we are safe; for every petition of Mary is heard and she can never meet with a repulse.

(*Affections, prayers, visit with Mary*)

V.

Charity is not inflated (1 Cor 13:4 — Humility)

He who loves Jesus is not vain about his own worth but humbles himself and accepts humiliation.

A proud person is like a balloon filled with air which seems great; but that greatness, in reality, is nothing more than a little air which is quickly dispersed as soon as the balloon is opened. He who loves God is humble and does not inflate his own worth because of anything of value in himself — he knows that whatever he possesses is a gift from God.

Two things are chiefly requisite for the stability of a house — the foundation and the roof. The foundation in us must be humility, that is, in acknowledging ourselves good for nothing and capable of nothing if left to ourselves. The roof is the divine assistance in which alone we ought to put our trust.

Whenever we find ourselves unusually favored by God, we must humble ourselves the more. The more a soul realizes it is unworthy, the more God enriches it with graces. When a soul loves God and cordially repents of having offended him, he forgets all past infidelities, as he reminds us through the Prophet Ezekiel: "If the wicked man turns away from all the sins he has committed . . . none of the crimes he committed shall be remembered against him" (Ezk 18:21-22).

From the saints we learn that a single act of humility is worth more than all the riches of the universe. We, too, must act in this manner if we would save our souls and keep ourselves in the grace of God till death, reposing all our confidence in God alone. The proud man relies on his own strength, and falls on that account. The humble man, by placing his trust in God alone, stands firm and falls not, however violent and multiplied the temptations may be. His watchword is, "I have the strength for everything through him who empowers me" (Ph 4:13).

Some are tempted by presumption — as if they were strong enough by themselves to withstand all temptation. But if God were to withdraw his graces for but an instant, we would be lost.

Some are tempted by despair — as if nothing could save them, not even the grace of God. With the Psalmist let us cry out, "In you, O Lord, I take refuge; let me never be put to shame. In your justice rescue me" (Ps 31:2).

"Learn from me," says the Lord, "for I am meek and humble of heart" (Mt 11:29). Our Lord gave us the example of humility when he was rejected by his contemporaries. Some will admit in prayer that they are great sinners, but let someone else look down upon them as a sinner, and reject them, and they become angry. That is humility of tongue but not of heart. People who resent being slighted are far from perfection.

How is it possible not to love humility when we see how our God was spit upon and buffeted during his Passion? "Then they spat in his face and struck him, while some slapped him" (Mt 26:67). This is why the Church wants us to keep the Crucifix above our altars that we may always remember how he accepted humiliation. What an example for us!

If a person pretending to spirituality practices prayer, makes frequent Communions, fasts, and mortifies himself and yet cannot put up with an affront, or a biting word, of what is it a sign? It is a sign that he is a hollow cane, without humility and without virtue. If you cannot endure cuffs and blows for God, at least endure a passing word.

It is scandalous for one who receives Holy Communion frequently to resent every little word of contempt or criticism. How edifying, on the other hand, when that person answers with mildness and tries to make peace with the critic. Sometimes it might even be better to remain silent in the face of criticism. It is better when we do not complain to others about these slights, these hurt feelings.

The *Imitation of Christ* contains several examples of humility: "What others say commands an attentive hearing and what you say shall have no notice taken of it. Others shall make a request and obtain it; you shall ask for something and be refused. Others shall be praised by men but for you no one says a word. Such and such an honor will be conferred on others but you shall be passed over as unfit for anything.

"With such trials the Lord may test and probe his faithful servant, to see how far he has learned to overcome himself and to hold his peace. Nature indeed will not like it; but you will derive immense profit thereby, if you support it all in silence" (Bk 3, c. 49).

Our Lord called such a person "blessed." "Blessed are you when they insult you and persecute you and utter every kind of evil against you falsely because of me. Rejoice and be glad for your reward will be great in heaven" (Mt 5:11-12).

The grand occasion for practicing humility is when being corrected by a superior or someone else. The worldly prickle at that and come with denials and excuses. They consider the critic an enemy. When the humble man is corrected he is sorry that he committed the fault. The proud man, on the other hand, is sorry that he was caught.

There is one case where self-defense must be used. That is when it must be used to prevent scandal or the appearance of scandal. To keep silent when falsely accused at other times is a source of great merit and spiritual progress. As a matter of fact it leads to greater freedom of spirit because it means that the person rises above what the world thinks of him or her.

(Affections, prayers, visit to Mary)

VI.

Charity is not ambitious
(1 Cor 13:5 — Vainglory)

He who loves Jesus Christ desires nothing more.

He who loves God does not seek to be esteemed and honored by his fellow men. The single desire of his heart is to enjoy the favor of Almighty God who alone forms the object of his love.

Those who seek earthly honors soon put aside humility and then follow other vices. St. James reminds us, "God resists the proud but gives grace to the humble" (Jm 4:6). Thus, when we hear of the fall of some of the towering cedars of Lebanon such as a Saul, Solomon, or Tertullian, it is a sign that they did not give themselves totally to God. Beware, then, when the world heaps praise on you, and turn to God with true humility.

Be especially on guard against all ambitious seeking of preference and about sensibility over points of honor. Some are striving to be better than others, even with the semblance of devotion, but if their honor is touched, they lose their peace of mind and the practice of spiritual matters. The true lover of God is happy to be overlooked by others, and does not worry if he is held in small repute.

The saying of St. Francis of Assisi is most true: "What I am before God, that I am." Of what use is it to pass for great in the eyes of the world, if before God we are vile and worthless? As St. Augustine puts it, "The approbation of him who praises neither heals a bad conscience, nor does the reproach of one who blames wound a good conscience."

Oh, what security is found in the hidden life for those who wish to love Jesus Christ cordially! Christ set the example himself by living hidden and unknown for thirty years in a workshop. For this very reason, the Desert Fathers hid themselves in deserts and caves. For this reason people entered hermitages and today enter enclosed contemplative monasteries and convents.

Whoever, then, would make great progress in the love of Jesus Christ must absolutely deal a death-blow to the love of self-esteem. We must avoid all ambition of appearing in public and of making a parade in the eyes of others. We must shun with even greater caution the ambition of governing others.

St. Mary Magdalene de Pazzi said: "The honor of a spiritual person consists in being put below and in abhorring all superiority over others. The ambition of a soul that loves God should be to excel all others in humility according to the counsel of St. Paul, 'humbly regard others as more important than yourselves'" (Ph 2:3).

In a word, whoever loves God must make God the sole object of his ambition.

(Affections, prayer, visit to Mary)

VII.

Charity seeks not it own interests
(1 Cor 13:5 — Detachment)

*He who loves Jesus seeks to detach
himself from every creature.*

Whoever desires to love Jesus Christ with his whole heart must banish from his heart all that is not God, but is merely self-love. That is the meaning of the words, "seeks not its own interests," not to seek ourselves but only what pleases God.

This is what God requires of us: "You shall love the Lord, your God, with all your heart, with all your soul, and with all your mind" (Mt 22:37). Two things are needed to love God with our whole heart:

1. To clear it of earth.
2. To fill it with holy love.

It follows that a heart in which selfish, earthly affections linger can never fully belong to God. Mortification, self-denial, and detachment from selfish attraction to creatures are the ways to clear the heart of earth.

The mistake that some make is that, even though they wish to become saints, they want to do it in their own way. They do not want to forsake vanity in dress, delicacies in food or human prerogatives. They continue to want honors and offices, they are impatient in illness and grow despondent over crosses, they continue to be attached to the sensible goods of the earth. The world makes so much noise that they cannot hear the words of God.

There is a story that says Tiberius Caesar wanted to enroll Jesus Christ in the Roman Pantheon and honor him along with the other gods. The Roman Senate refused on the ground that he was too proud a god and wanted to be worshipped alone, without any companions.

It is quite true. God will be alone the subject of our adoration and love, not from pride but because it is his just due — and because, too, of the love he bears for us. He is a jealous God because he loves us exceedingly and wants a return of love. "Or do you suppose," writes St. James, "that the scripture speaks without meaning when it says, 'The spirit that he has made to dwell in us tends towards jealousy?'" (Jm 4:5).

The Lord in the Song of Songs praises his spouse, saying: "You are an enclosed garden, my sister, my bride, an enclosed garden, a fountain sealed" (Sg 4:12). He calls her an enclosed garden because the soul bound to him by religious vows keeps her heart shut against every selfish, earthly love in order to preserve all for God alone.

And does Jesus Christ really deserve all our love? Ah, too much, too much has he deserved it, both for his own goodness and for his love for us.

David longed to have wings free from all ties to earth in order to fly away and repose in God. "Had I but wings like a dove I would fly away and be at rest" (Ps 55:7). Many souls would like to fly to the heights of God's love but even though they practice many virtues, pray, and receive Holy Communion often, they do not have the courage to detach themselves from frivolous attachments and so they never lift a foot from the ground.

St. John of the Cross remarked: "It signifies little if a bird is tied to the ground by a slight thread or a thick rope. It remains unable to fly." St. John of the Cross remarked that it "is a pitiful thing indeed, to see certain souls, rich in spiritual exercises, who do not attain divine union because of some trifling attachment to things of the earth."

Our Lord told his followers when speaking of the grace of discipleship, "Everyone of you who does not renounce all his possessions cannot be my disciple" (Lk 14:33). The Desert Fathers took him literally and went off into solitude. Others have learned to be detached from worldly goods even while they must administer them.

Our heart is quite too small to love this God, so loving and so lovely, and who merits an infinite love. Shall we then think of dividing this one little heart between creatures and God?

As in the case of St. Thomas Aquinas and many other saints, when they announced to family and friends that they wanted to enter the religious life, they faced tremendous opposition. In this case, the person must obey the call of God over the virtue of obedience to parents.

On the other hand, think of those who have entered clerical life just to please parents or relatives. A true vocation to the sublime dignity of Holy Orders is distinguished by three signs:

1. The requisite knowledge;
2. The intention of applying one's life only to God's service; and
3. Positive goodness of life.

I will speak to this last point:

The Council of Trent has prescribed to Bishops to raise to Holy Orders only those whose irreproachable conduct has been proved. While this refers directly to external proof, certainly the more important is the interior disposition. Thus the Council adds that those to be admitted to Holy Orders must show themselves worthy by a wise maturity.

Religious enter religious communities in order to perfect themselves and grow in virtue, step by step. Since the priest is called to represent Jesus Christ in a special way, he must acquire sanctity before he advances in Holy Orders. Sinful habits must be overcome before one presents himself for ordination.

Moreover, anyone who would belong wholly to God must be free of all human respect. How many there are who do good works but want all the world to know about it. They long for public notice and want the praise of the worldly.

How different the saints! They would rather publish their defects and pass as miserable creatures. When they perform any act of virtue, they prefer that only God know and approve.

But of all things, self-detachment is most necessary, that is detachment from self-will. Succeed in subduing yourself and you will easily triumph in every other combat. "Conquer yourself" was the motto St. Francis Xavier drew from Our Lord's statement, "Whoever wishes to come after me must deny himself, take up his cross, and follow me" (Mt 16:24).

The power to conquer ourselves by denying self-will is truly a great grace. Selfishness is surely the road to hell. St. Bernard wrote that it has the power to take the goodness out of good works. Unhappy the man who lives as a slave to self-will.

St. James asks: "Where do the wars and where do the conflicts among you come from? Is it not from your passions that make war within your members. You covet but you do not possess. . . ." Appetite for sensual delights, covetousness of riches, ambitiously seeking honors and self-will — these cause the conflicts within us and around us.

Some souls are spiritually troubled because they cannot do good works for their own pleasure. The inability to gratify self-will is so often the cause of the trouble.

Therefore, we must love God in the way that please him and not in what pleases us. God will have the soul emptied of all in order to be united to himself and be replenished with his divine love.

St. Teresa begins her work, *The Interior Castle*, with this same thought: "One thing is certain, that the more completely we empty ourselves of creatures by detaching ourselves from them for the love of God, the more abundantly will he fill us with himself, and the more closely shall we be united with him."

St. Catherine of Genoa says: "The trials that God allows into our lives are absolutely necessary; his purpose is to consume in us, by means of them, all irregular movements, both within and without. Want of resignation in these trials stands in the way of divine union. Indeed, until we find these trials sweet for the sake of God, we shall never arrive at divine union."

Those who truly love Jesus must be stripped of all unworthy earthly affections in order to keep affection for Jesus in first place.

Finally, I ask: What is meant by giving the soul entirely to God? It means:

1. To shun whatever may be displeasing to God and to do what is most pleasing to him.
2. To accept unreservedly all that comes from his hand no matter how hard or disagreeable it may be.
3. To give preference in all things to the will of God over our own.

(Affections, prayers, visit to Mary)

VIII.

Charity is not quick-tempered
(1 Cor 13:5 — Meekness)

*Whoever loves Jesus Christ is never angry
with his neighbor.*

We have spoken much about meekness, and one of its offspring is the ability to control anger in the contrarieties that surround us. Here we will make some practical suggestions.

Our Lord valued meekness and humility for he said, "Learn of me, for I am meek and humble of heart" (Mt 11:29). He was the "Lamb of God" (Jn 1:29) who went silently and meekly to his sacrificial death. When he stood silently before his persecutors in the house of Caiaphas (Jn 18:23), he was struck by the high priest's servant. And on the Cross he forgave: "Father, forgive them, they know not what they do" (Lk 23:34).

How dear to Jesus Christ are those meek souls who, in suffering affronts, derisions, calumnies, persecutions, and even blows, are not irritated against the person who so injures or strikes them!

God is always pleased with the prayers of the meek. Their prayers are always heard. Heaven is expressly promised to the meek: "Blessed are the meek, for they shall inherit the land" (Mt 5:5). What is this land but Heaven, our true homeland?

In order to remain constantly united with Jesus Christ we must do all with tranquillity. We must not be troubled by any contradiction we may encounter. The Lord does not abide in troubled hearts. St. Francis de Sales in his *Introduction to the Devout Life* (3:8) talks about this subject at length:

"Never put yourself in a passion or open the door to anger on any pretext. Once it gains entrance it is no longer in our power to check it or moderate it as we wish. The remedies against it are:

1. To check it immediately by diverting the mind to some other object, and to say not a word;
2. Imitate the Apostles when they saw the storm at sea and have recourse to the Lord, to whom it belongs to restore peace to the soul; and
3. If you feel that, owing to your weakness, anger has entered in, do violence to yourself to regain your composure and then follow that by some kind word to the one who irritated you."

St. Francis de Sales confessed that two passions bothered him, anger and love. He remarked that it took twenty-two years to overcome the anger, but that he had overcome worldly love by changing its object from creatures to God.

Sometimes we think we can relieve our anger by giving vent to it, but this always leaves the soul troubled. Even ill-humor can undermine our peace of soul. Certainly you must not go to rest with ill-humor in your heart. Divert yourself by reading, music, or a conversation with a friend.

This inner tranquillity does not come easily and needs effort to maintain. However, as we feel an increased tenderness towards Jesus Christ we will grow in gentleness and meekness. When we encounter anger in others, it is most important to respond with gentleness. St. John Chrysostom said that it is not right to answer the fire that burns in another with the fire of an indignant or sarcastic reply.

There may be times when our anger is justified, but it is very difficult to know exactly when and where. Therefore, it is much better to reply with gentleness and without resentment. The safest way is to remain silent or gentle, and return to the matter when both parties have cooled down.

Do not forget that we must practice meekness with ourselves. If we get angry with ourselves, we keep our souls in a troubled state. Such self-anger comes from the devil, self-love, or the good opinion we have of ourselves.

Meekness is most especially necessary when we have to correct others. Corrections made with bitter zeal often do more harm than good, especially if the one corrected is excited. Better to wait for a more opportune time. If we are excited or ill-tempered when we correct someone, that person will not pay attention, attributing it to our ill-humor.

(*Affections, prayers, visit to Mary*)

IX.

Charity does not brood over injury, does not rejoice over wrong-doing, but rejoices with the truth. (1 Cor 13:5-6 — Conformity to God's Will)

*Whoever loves Jesus Christ only desires
what Jesus Christ desires.*

Charity and truth always go together. Charity, conscious that God is the only one and true good, detests iniquity which is directly opposed to the divine will; it takes satisfaction only in what pleases God. The soul that loves God is heedless of what people say and only aims at pleasing God.

As Blessed Henry Suso said, "That man stands with God who strives to conform himself to the truth and, for the rest, is utterly indifferent to the opinion or treatment of mankind."

A. THE NECESSITY OF CONFORMING TO THE WILL OF GOD

If we want to become saints our whole endeavor should be, never to follow our own will, but always to follow the will of God. The substance of all the precepts and divine counsels is comprised in doing and suffering what God wills and in the manner he wills it. We ask God to give us a holy liberty of spirit which leads us to embrace whatever is pleasing to Jesus Christ regardless of human feelings.

St. Augustine says, "Love and do what you like." Whoever really loves God seeks only to please him; all his pleasure is in that. People who are in love with each other seek only to please the beloved. The more perfect the love, the more ardent is the desire to please. If this is true of love between human beings, it is all the more true when dealing with divine love.

God wishes us to love him with our whole heart: "You shall love the Lord, your God, with all your heart, with all your soul and with all your mind" (Mt 22:37). That person loves Jesus who says to him with St. Paul, "Lord, what do you want me to do?" (Ac 9:6). St. Vincent de Paul said, "Conformity with the will of God is the treasure of a Christian." We know it is pleasing to God, for he told us "not a hair of your head will be destroyed" (Lk 21:18).

But this conformity to the divine will must be entire, without any reserve, and constant, without withdrawal. In this consists the height of perfection, and to this (I repeat) all our works, all our desires, and all our prayers ought to tend.

Some people, given to prayer, on reading of the ecstasies and raptures of saints like Teresa of Avila and Philip Neri, wish to enjoy these supernatural gifts themselves. Banish such wishes as contrary to humility. If we really wish to become saints we must aspire after true union with God, which is to unite our will entirely to the will of God. In the words of St. Teresa, "Those people are deceived who fancy that union with God consists in ecstasies, raptures and sensible enjoyments."

If we were conformed to the will of God in every trouble, we should undoubtedly become saints and be the happiest of people. This then should be the chief object of our attention, to keep our will in unbroken union with the will of God in every occurrence of life, be it pleasant or unpleasant.

In the *Imitation of Christ* we read "that he is not deserving of the name of lover who is not ready to endure all things for his beloved and to follow in all things the will of his beloved." Whoever, then, resigns himself to the divine will in troubles, travels to God post-haste.

As St. Teresa observes, "What greater acquisition can we make than to have some proof that we are pleasing God?" To this I add, that we cannot have a more certain proof of this than by peacefully embracing the crosses which God sends us. We please God by thanking him for his benefits on earth. "But," says John of Avila, "one 'Blessed be God!' uttered in adversity is worth six thousand acts of thanksgiving offered in prosperity."

The crosses we bear come in many forms. Some are directly

allowed by God, such as illness, scanty talents, accidents, reversals of fortune and the like. Others come indirectly from God through our fellow men, such as persecutions, thefts, injury, jealousy, contempt, false words, rumor and gossip. We embrace these crosses whether they come for chastisement, correction, or purification.

Certain souls are greedy for spiritual dainties in prayer and tender feelings. Courageous souls that seek sincerely to belong wholly to God, ask him only for the light to understand his will and for the strength to put it into practice.

B. OBEDIENCE

What is the surest way to know the will of God? There is no surer way than by obedience to religious superiors and placing oneself under a spiritual director. God is more pleased with the sacrifice which we make to him of our own will, by submitting it to obedience, than with all the other sacrifices which we can offer him.

In other things, such as almsgiving, fasting, mortifications and the like, we give of what is ours to God, but in giving him our will, we give him everything. When we say to God, "O Lord, make me know by means of obedience what you want of me, for I wish to comply with it all," we have nothing more to offer him.

It is a delusion to think that anyone can possibly be better employed than in the discharge of what obedience has imposed. To interrupt something given in obedience to spend an hour in prayer is actually to withdraw from God because of self-will.

The Blessed Mother once revealed to St. Bridget that he who relinquishes some mortification through obedience reaps a twofold profit; first of all, he has already obtained the merit of the mortification by the good-will to do it, and, secondly, he also gains the merit of obedience by foregoing it.

For obedience to be perfect, we must obey with the will and with the judgment. To obey with the will signifies to obey willingly and not by constraint, after the fashion of slaves. To obey with the judgment means to conform our judgment to that of the superior, without examining what is commanded. This holds good not merely for religious but likewise for the laity living under obedience to a spiritual director.

(*Editor's note: St. Alphonsus is talking about the virtue of obedience in the context of seeking spiritual perfection. Obviously, the superior or spiritual director cannot command anything sinful or morally offensive. The suspension of judgment he speaks of does not in any way excuse the person from refusing anything sinful. That sort of judgment cannot be suspended. The author is writing with the understanding that both parties are seeking true Christian holiness.*)

We can sum up this chapter this way. Our salvation and perfection consist in:

1. Denying self-will.
2. Following the will of God.
3. Praying that he always give us the strength to do both.

(*Affections, prayers and visit to Mary*)

X.

Charity Bears All Things
(1 Cor 13:7 — Patience)

Whoever loves Jesus bears all thing for Jesus Christ including illness, poverty and contempt.

In Chapter One we spoke of the virtue of patience. Here we will treat of some occasions that call for the practice of that virtue.

Father Balthazar Alvarez said that a Christian need not imagine himself to have made any progress until he has succeeded in penetrating his heart with a lasting sense of the sorrows, poverty, and ignominies of Jesus Christ so as to support with loving patience every sort of sorrow, privation and contempt for the sake of Jesus Christ.

A. PATIENCE IN SICKNESS

First let us consider bodily infirmities which, when borne with patience, merit for us a beautiful crown.

Saints such as Vincent de Paul, Francis de Sales (*Editor's note: and St. Alphonsus*) suffered many infirmities, yet they constantly gave such good example of peace and serenity that most people thought they enjoyed good health always. When they were ill, they reported to their physicians, took the prescribed medicines and then remained at peace, never uttering any complaints.

What a contrast to this is the conduct of those who do nothing but complain even for the most trifling indisposition, and who want their family and friends to gather around them for sympathy. As St. Teresa told her nuns, "My sisters, learn to suffer something for the love of Jesus Christ without letting all the world know of it."

Someone who is sick may say, "It's not so much the infirmity that afflicts me, but it's that it keeps me from going to Mass and performing my devotions in Church." If you are resigned to the will of God, accept that it is his desire that you embrace patiently your infirmities. In the words of John of Avila, "If you seek the will of God, what does it matter to you whether you are well or ill?"

But you say that you cannot even pray because of a headache. So be it: you cannot meditate, but why can you not make acts of resignation to the will of God? If you would only make those acts you could not offer a better prayer, welcoming with love all that comes your way.

St. Teresa wrote, "When I remember in how many ways my Savior suffered, though he was innocence itself, I don't know how it could enter my mind to complain of my sufferings." Once when she was seriously ill, our Lord appeared to her, covered with wounds, and said, "Behold, my daughter, the bitterness of my sufferings and consider if yours equal mine."

Consider the martyrs who underwent such cruel tortures, many with great joy because they were found worthy to die for Christ and merit the crown of glory. Did they act this way because they were insensitive to pain or weak in intellect? "No," says St. Bernard, "not insensibility but love caused this."

Above all, in time of sickness we should be ready to accept death and the kind of death that God pleases to mete out to us. We must die and our life must finish in our last illness — and we do not know which will be our last illness. If we truly love God, we should ardently long to go to see him and love him with all our strength in Paradise.

B. PATIENCE IN POVERTY

In the second place we must practice patience in enduring poverty. Our patience is certainly very much tried when we are in need of temporal goods. But as St. Augustine said, "He who has not God has nothing; he who has God has all." Consider St. Francis of Assisi, barefoot, clad in sackcloth, deprived of all material things, yet he was happier than all the reigning monarchs in the world. A poor man who has nothing, desires nothing and is content in his poverty, is rich indeed.

The true lovers of God have nothing and yet have everything — since, when temporal goods fail them, they exclaim: "My Jesus, you alone are sufficient for me," and with that they rest satisfied. Let our solicitude be not for earthly goods, but for those of Paradise, which are immeasurably greater and last forever.

St. Bernard reminds us, "The avaricious man hungers after earthly things as a beggar; the poor man despises them as a lord." The miser is always hungry as a beggar because he is never satiated with the possessions he desires; the poor man, on the contrary, despises them all as a rich lord, inasmuch as he desires nothing.

The love of poverty should be especially precious to religious, who take the vow. However, some want the honor of poverty, not the inconvenience. In the words of St. Bernard, "Many religious wish to be poor; but on the condition of wanting for nothing."

Our Lord once told Angela of Foligno, "If poverty were not of great excellence I would not have chosen it for myself, nor have bequeathed it to my elect."

> *(Editor's note: St. Alphonsus is addressing himself to the virtue of poverty in the context of pursuing holiness. He is not addressing the social justice question of the impoverished who must be patient in the face of hunger, homelessness and economic deprivation. The Christian has the duty of working to alleviate these conditions. It has been pointed out that Christ blessed the poor in spirit, not poverty as such.)*

C. PATIENCE UNDER CONTEMPT

In the third place, we must practice patience and show our love of God by tranquilly submitting to contempt.

When anyone decides to pursue the spiritual life, he can expect insults, opposition and even persecution. These must be borne with tranquillity of spirit. Some of the saints even learned to long for them as a way of showing their love for God.

St. Teresa reminds us, "Whoever aspires to perfection must beware of ever saying: 'They had no right to treat me so.' If you will not bear any cross but one which is based on reason, then perfection is not for you."

In sum, affronts, poverty, torments and all tribulations serve only to drive that soul away from God who does not love God. When they happen to a soul who loves God they become an instrument of closer union with God and more ardent love of God. However great and grievous trouble may be, so far from extinguishing the flames of charity, they only serve to enkindle them the more in a soul who loves nothing else but God.

Does God take pleasure in sending us crosses? No, he is no tyrant but a true lover. He sees that these sufferings purify us, strengthen us and let us exercise various virtues. It is something like a mother who weans her child by putting gall on her breast.

"We know that all things work for good for those who love God" (Rm 8:28).

(Affections, prayers, visit to Mary)

XI.

Charity Believes All Things
(1 Cor 13:7 — Faith)

He who loves Jesus Christ believes all his words.

Whoever loves a person believes all that he says. Consequently, the more a soul loves Jesus Christ, the more lively and unshakable his or her faith.

When the good thief beheld our Redeemer, though he was innocent, suffering death upon the cross with such patience, he began at once to love him. Under the influence of this love, and of the divine light which then broke upon his soul, he believed that this was truly the Son of God. He then begged not to be forgotten by him when he should have passed into his Kingdom.

Faith is the foundation of charity, but faith afterwards receives its perfection from charity. Our faith comes alive through works of charity. His faith is most perfect whose love of God is most perfect. Charity produces in us not merely the faith of the understanding (intellect) but the faith of the will also.

Those who believe only with the intellect — as is the case with sinners who are perfectly convinced of the truths of the faith but do not choose to live according to the divine commandments — such as these have a very weak faith. Had they a more lively belief that the grace of God is a priceless treasure, and that sin, because it robs us of this grace, is the worst of evils, they would certainly change their lives.

On the other hand, he who believes not only with the intellect but also with the will, so that he not only believes, but has the will to believe in God, the revealer of truth, from the love he has for him, and rejoices in so believing —such a one has perfect faith and consequently seeks to make his life conformable to the truths that he believes.

The weakness of the faith of many persons is to be traced to the wickedness of their living. Rather than forego the enjoyment of forbidden pleasures he scorns the divine friendship and pretends that the commandments do not bind. He strives to blind himself to the eternal truths of death, judgment, Hell and divine justice. The next step is to deny the immortality of the soul and the existence of God. Thus he can live like a brute beast, without laws and without reason.

This laxity of morals is the real reason behind the spate of books and systems on Materialism, Indifferentism, Politicism, Deism, and Naturalism. Some deny the existence of God, or the existence of Divine Providence; some promote absolute predestination which teaches that God creates some souls to be damned for all eternity.

Oh, the ingratitude and wickedness of mankind! God has created them in his mercy to make them eternally happy in Heaven; he has poured out on them so many lights, benefits, and graces to bring them to eternal life. This is why he redeemed them at the price of so many sorrows and sufferings. Yet they strive to deny it all that they may give free rein to their vicious inclinations! Struggle as they will, however, the unhappy beings cannot wrest themselves from remorse of conscience and the dread of divine vengeance.

The true lover of Jesus Christ keeps the eternal truths constantly in view and orders all his actions according to them. How well he understands the words of the wise man, "Vanity of vanities; all things are vanity!" (Ec 1:2). All earthly greatness is mere smoke, dirt and delusion. The soul's only welfare and happiness consists in loving its Creator and in doing his blessed will.

We are, in reality, no more than what we are before God. It is of no use to gain the whole world if the soul is lost. All the goods in the whole world cannot satisfy the human heart. Only God can. In truth, we must leave all in order to gain all.

There are some lukewarm Christians who believe in the truths of divine Revelation, but do not believe all. They say, "Blessed are those who have money and power, who do not have to suffer, who avoid persecutions and crosses." This is not the Gospel of Jesus Christ.

The true believer believes all that is said in the Gospel, and has a real love for Jesus Christ.

(Affections, prayers and visit to Mary)

XII.

Charity hopes all things (1 Cor 13:7 — Hope)

Whoever loves Jesus Christ hopes for all things from him.

Hope increases charity, and charity increases hope.

Hope in the divine goodness undoubtedly gives an increase to our love of Jesus Christ. St. Thomas tells us that when we hope to receive some benefit from a person, we begin to love him. On this account, the Lord forbids us to put our trust in creatures: "Put not your trust in princes" (Ps 146:2). Or again, "Cursed is the man who trusts in human beings" (Jr 17:5).

St. Vincent de Paul said, "Let us beware of reposing too much confidence in men. When God beholds us thus leaning on them for support, he himself withdraws from us." On the other hand, the more we trust in God the more shall we advance in his holy love. "They that hope in the Lord will renew their strength, they will soar as with eagle's wings; they will run and not grow weary, walk and not grow faint" (Is 40:31).

Now as hope increases the love of God, so does love help to increase hope. Charity makes us the adopted sons and daughters of God. In the natural order we are the work of his hands; in the supernatural order we are made children of God and partakers of the divine nature through the merits of Jesus Christ. As St. Peter writes, "He has bestowed on us the precious and very great promises, so that through them you may come to share in the divine nature" (2 P 1:4).

If charity makes us the sons and daughters of God, it consequently makes us heirs of Heaven according to St. Paul: "And if children, then heirs, heirs of God and joint heirs with Christ" (Rm 8:17). These tremendous ties that bind us to God in love increase our hope for the life of Heaven. No wonder the saints would repeat the line, "Your kingdom come, Your kingdom come!"

The primary object of Christian hope is God, whom the soul enjoys in the kingdom of Heaven. The hope of Paradise is inseparably connected with charity which there receives its full and complete perfection. Charity is that infinite treasure, spoken of by the wise man, which makes us friends of God: "An unfailing treasure; those who gain this treasure win the friendship of God" (Ws 7:14).

St. Thomas Aquinas says that friendship is founded on the mutual communication of goods. Friendship is nothing more than a mutual love between friends — so it follows that there must be a reciprocal interchange of the good which each possesses. In his words, "If there is no communication there is no friendship." That is why Christ said to his disciples, "I have called you friends, because I have told you everything I have heard from my Father" (Jn 15:15). Since he had made them his friends, he had communicated all his secrets to them.

St. Thomas teaches us that charity does not exclude the desire of the reward prepared for us in Heaven by Almighty God. On the contrary, it makes us look to it as the chief object of our love, for such is God who constitutes the bliss of Paradise. Friendship implies that friends rejoice with one another.

In Heaven the soul belongs wholly to God and God belongs wholly to the soul according to the measure of its capacity and merits. The soul rejoices at the glory which God imparts to it but for the sole purpose of referring it back to God himself, and so doing its best to increase the divine glory.

That is why St. Thomas defines hope as the "sure expectation of eternal happiness." Its certainty arises from the infallible promise of God to give eternal life to his faithful servants. Now charity, by taking away sin, at the same time takes away all obstacles to our obtaining the happiness of the blessed. Therefore, the greater our charity the greater also and firmer is our hope.

(Affections, prayers, visit to Mary)

XIII.

Charity endures all things
(1 Cor 13:7 — Temptation)

Whoever loves Jesus Christ with a strong love does not cease to love him in the midst of temptations and desolations.

A. TEMPTATIONS

Of all the afflictions that a loving soul must face, one of the most difficult is the struggle against inner temptations.

1. Why does God permit temptations?

Temptations do not come from God for "God himself tempts no one" (Jm 1:13). Temptations come from the world, the flesh, and the devil. Nevertheless, God does at times permit his most cherished souls to be the most grievously tempted.

In the first place, God allows it in order that from temptations the soul may better learn its own weakness and the need for divine assistance not to fall. During times of consolation the soul feels that it can conquer every assault and achieve everything for the greater glory of God.

But when the soul is strongly tempted and reeling on the brink of the precipice, then it becomes better acquainted with its own misery and the realization that it cannot resist unless God comes to the rescue. Listen to St. Paul: "That I might not become too elated by the abundance of revelations, a thorn in the flesh was given to me, an angel of Satan, to beat me, to keep me from being too elated" (2 Cor 12:7).

God also permits temptations with the view of detaching us more thoroughly from this life and enkindling in us the desire to go and be with him in Heaven. Some pious souls, finding themselves attacked day and night cry out, "Woe is me that my sojourn is prolonged" (Ps 120:5). They sigh for the moment when they can say, "Broken was the snare and we were freed" (Ps 124:7).

Almighty God also permits us to be tempted to make us grow richer in merits, as was said to Tobias, "When you did not hesitate [to do good works] I was sent to test you" (Tob 12:13). Never think you have lost God's favor because of temptations.

Sometimes the devil tries to confuse us into thinking that the temptation is the sin. Be the thoughts and imaginations ever so vile and violent, they are never sinful unless we consent to them. By resisting mightily the soul grows stronger, more single-minded and dearer to God. In the words of St. Bernard: "As often as we conquer, so often are we crowned."

Nor must we be disturbed if evil thoughts persist. All that matters is that we do not consent to them and try to rid our mind of them. "God is faithful and will not let you be tried beyond your strength; but with the trial he will also provide a way out, so that you may be able to bear it" (1 Cor 10:13).

Because of this extra grace, we may actually derive great profit from these temptations. This is why God frequently allows even his best friends to undergo temptations that they may turn them into a source of greater merit on earth and of greater glory in Heaven.

Stagnant water soon becomes putrid. A soul too much at ease, without struggle or temptation stands in great danger of stagnating. Faced with trials, the soul in love with God turns to him fervently for greater strength.

This does not mean that we should seek temptations. On the contrary, Jesus Christ taught us to pray in the Lord's Prayer, "Lead us not into temptation" (Mt 6:13). When, by God's permission, we are tried, we must not become alarmed or discouraged. We must rely wholly on Jesus and beg for his help. St. Augustine says, "Throw yourself on him and do not be afraid; he will not withdraw to let you fall."

2. Remedies against temptation

Spiritual masters describe many remedies to vanquish temptations, but I will speak of only one here. Have immediate recourse to God with all humility and confidence, saying, "Deign, O Lord to rescue; O Lord, make haste to help me" (Ps 70:2).

We cannot doubt that God will help us as he promises so many times in the Scriptures. Did Our Lord not say, "Come to me all you who labor and are burdened and I will give you rest" (Mt 11:28)?

The Psalmist also attests to this: "Then call upon me in time of distress and I will rescue you, and you will honor me" (Ps 50:15); "I call upon you and you will answer me, O God" (Ps 17:6); "Praised be the Lord, I exclaim and I am safe from my enemies" (Ps 18:4); and "The Lord is near to all who call upon him, to all who call upon him in truth" (Ps 145:18). To which St. Paul adds: "The same Lord is the Lord of all, enriching all who call upon him" (Rm 10:12).

When it comes to temptations against the faith or in matters of sexuality, do not meet them head on, directly. That merely keeps them in mind the more. Act immediately to get rid of them indirectly by making acts of love of God. We should then apply ourselves to some indifferent occupation which will distract us.

Those who do try to live a virtuous life over a long period of time may be sure that if there is a doubt about whether they have consented to temptation, the doubt is in their favor. Their good will is to be presumed. Those of scrupulous conscience must follow their confessor's advice and put their trust fully in God.

If I seem to repeat myself on the necessity of prayer, it is because it is the most important remedy I know of in time of temptation. Remember to turn to Mary, too, since as St. Bernard says, "God has willed us to receive nothing that has not passed through the hands of Mary."

(Affections, prayers and visit to Mary)

B. DESOLATIONS

St. Francis de Sales (*Introduction to the Devout Life*, 4:13) teaches us that "it is a mistake to estimate devotions by the consolations which we feel. True devotion in the way of God consists in having a determined will to execute all that is pleasing to God."

God sometimes uses the route of desolation to draw souls to him, to help them overcome inordinate attachment to their own wills. They must first learn detachment from earthly goods and honors, but then they may well have to become detached from the consolations of prayer.

With a view to produce a fondness for spiritual things, God regales the soul at first with great consolations, to wean her away from the gratifications of sense. But the soul's attachment to God at this point is imperfect, inasmuch as it is fostered more by that sensibility of spiritual consolations than by the real wish to do what is pleasing to God. When God deigns to let us feel the presence of his grace, let us thankfully receive them, but let us beware of settling down on them.

But God wishes to see the soul purified and divested of all sensible satisfaction, in order to unite her entirely to himself by means of pure love. He thus puts the soul in the crucible of desolation, uncertain if she is in God's grace and assailed by temptations. When a soul that loves God finds herself in this state, she must not lose courage.

St. John of the Cross wrote the following words of comfort to a desolate soul: "You were never in a better state than at present. You were never so deeply humbled, and so cut off from all attachment to the world. At the same time, you were never so thoroughly impressed with the conviction of your own wickedness. Neither were you ever so divested and purified of all self-seeking as now."

The saints of whom the Church sings are the choice stones which are reduced to shapeliness and beauty by the strokes of the chisel, that is, by temptations, by fears, by darkness and other torments, internal and external, until at length they are made worthy to be enthroned in the blessed kingdom of Paradise.

(Affections, prayers, visit to Mary)

Book Six

Novena to the Holy Spirit

Novena to the Holy Spirit

Consisting of meditations for each day of the novena
from the Feast of the Ascension till the eve of Pentecost.

The Novena to the Holy Spirit reflects the time of prayer that the Apostles and the most holy Mary spent in the Upper Room from the time of the Ascension until the descent of the Holy Spirit on Pentecost. In that sense it is the chief of all novenas.

The great gift bestowed on Pentecost was the gift of the Holy Spirit, a gift merited for us by the Passion of Jesus Christ himself. Jesus made this known when he said to the Apostles, "For if I do not go, the Advocate will not come to you, but if I go I will send him to you" (Jn 16:7).

Our faith teaches us that the Holy Spirit is the love that the Father and the Eternal Word bear one another. Therefore the gift of love, which the Lord infuses into our souls and which is the greatest of all gifts, is particularly attributed to the Holy Spirit, as St. Paul says, "because the love of God has been poured out into our hearts through the Holy Spirit that has been given to us" (Rm 5:5).

In this novena we will consider, above all, the great value of divine love in order that we may desire to obtain it. We will endeavor by devout exercise, and especially prayer, to be made partakers of it since God has promised it to those who ask with humility: "How much more will the Father in heaven give the Holy Spirit to those who ask him?" (Lk 11:13).

I.

Love is a fire that inflames the heart

God had ordered, in the ancient law, that there should be a fire kept continually burning on his altar: "And the fire is to be kept burning on the altar" (Lv 6:5). St. Gregory says that the altars of God are our hearts where he desires that the fire of his divine love should always be burning.

Not content with having given us his Son Jesus Christ to save us by his death, the Eternal Father also gave us the Holy Spirit that he might dwell in our souls and keep them constantly on fire with love.

Jesus himself declared that he had come into the world on purpose to inflame our hearts with this holy fire and that he desired nothing more than to see it kindled: "I have come to set the earth on fire and how I wish it were already blazing!" (Lk 12:49). Forgetting, therefore, the injuries and ingratitude he received from men on earth, when he had ascended into heaven he sent down upon us the Holy Spirit.

O most loving Redeemer, You love us as much in Your sufferings and ignominies as You do in Your kingdom of glory!

That is why the Holy Spirit chose to appear in the Upper Room under the form of tongues of fire: "Then there appeared to them tongues as of fire which parted and came to rest on each one of them"(Ac 2:3). And the Church responds in prayer, "May the Holy Spirit, we beg You, O Lord, inflame us with that fire which our Lord Jesus Christ came to cast upon the earth, and which he ardently desired should be enkindled."

This was the holy fire which has inflamed the saints to do such great things for God, to love their enemies, to desire contempt, to fast, and to embrace with delights even the tortures of martyrdom.

Love cannot remain idle and it never says, "It is enough." The soul that loves God, the more she does for the Beloved, the more she desires to do, in order to please him and to attract to herself his affections all the more.

This holy fire is enkindled by mental prayer: "In my thoughts a fire blazed forth" (Ps 39:4). If, therefore, we desire to burn with love towards God, let us love prayer; this is the blessed furnace in which this divine ardor is enkindled.

(Affections, prayers, visit to Mary)

II.

Love is a light that enlightens the soul

One of the greatest evils that the sin of Adam has produced in us is that darkening of our reason by means of the passions which cloud the mind. How miserable is that soul which allows itself to be ruled by any passion!

Passion is like a vapor, a veil which prevents us from seeing the truth. How can one fly from evil if he doesn't know what is evil? Besides, this obscurity increases in proportion as our sins increase.

The Holy Spirit, who is called "most blessed light," is he who not only inflames our hearts to love him, through his divine splendor, but also dispels our darkness and shows us the vanity of earthly things, the value of eternal goods, the importance of salvation, the price of grace, the goodness of God, the infinite love which he deserves, and the immense love he has for us.

"Now the natural person does not accept what pertains to the Spirit of God, for to him it is foolishness and he cannot understand it, because it is judged spiritually" (1 Cor 2:14). A man who is absorbed in the pleasures of earth knows little of these truths and therefore, unfortunate that he is, he loves what he ought to hate and hates what he ought to love.

St. Mary Magdalene de Pazzi exclaimed, "O love not known! O love not loved!" And St. Teresa said that God is not loved because he is not known. For that reason the saints were always seeking light from God.

"Send forth your light!" (Ps 43:3). "You indeed, O Lord, give light to my lamp; O my God, you brighten the darkness about me" (Ps 18:29). "Open my eyes that I may consider the wonders of your law" (Ps 119:18).

Yes, because without light we cannot avoid precipices nor can we find God.

(*Affections, prayers, visit to Mary*)

III.

Love is a fountain that satisfies

Love is also called a living fountain, fire, and charity. Our Blessed Redeemer said to the Samaritan woman, "Whoever drinks the water I shall give will never thirst; the water I shall give will become in him a spring of water welling up to eternal life" (Jn 4:14).

Love is the water which satisfies our thirst. He who loves God really with his whole heart neither seeks nor desires anything else, because in God he finds every good. Satisfied with God, he joyfully exclaims, "My God and my all!"

But the Almighty complains that many souls go about in search of fleeting and miserable pleasure and leave him who is the infinite good and fountain of all joy: "They have forsaken me, the source of living waters; they have dug themselves cisterns, broken cisterns that hold no water" (Jr 2:13).

Therefore, God, who loves us and desires to see us happy cries out and makes known to all, "Let anyone who thirsts come to me and drink" (Jn 7:37). Whoever wants to be happy, let him come to me and I will give him the Holy Spirit who will make him blessed both in this life and the next. "Whoever believes in me, as scripture says, 'Rivers of living water will flow from within him'" (Jn 7:38).

Therefore, whoever believes in Jesus Christ and loves him shall be enriched with so much grace that from his heart (the will) shall flow many fountains of holy virtues to save himself and give life to others. As St. John continues, "He said this in reference to the Spirit, that those who came to believe in him were to receive. There was, of course, no Spirit given yet because he had not been glorified" (Jn 7:39).

The key which opens these channels of blessed water is prayer which obtains every good for us in virtue of the promise, "Ask and you shall receive" (Jn 16:24). We are blind, poor and weak but prayer obtains for us light, strength, and an abundance of grace. God desires to give us his graces, but he wants us to pray for them.

(*Affections, prayers, visit to Mary*)

IV.

Love is a dew which makes fruitful

Love makes fruitful our good desires, our holy intentions, and our good works. These are the flowers and the fruits which the grace of the Holy Spirit produces.

Love is also called "dew" because it cools the heart of bad passions and temptations. Therefore the Holy Spirit is also called refreshment and a pleasing coolness. This dew descends into our hearts in time of prayer.

A quarter of an hour spent in prayer is sufficient to every movement of hatred or of inordinate love however ardent it may be.

Holy meditation is the place where love is set in order, so that we can love our neighbor as ourselves and God above everything.

Whoever loves God loves prayer, and whoever does not love prayer will find it morally impossible to overcome his passions.

(Affections, prayers and visit to Mary)

V.

Love is the rest that refreshes

In the hymn, *Veni, Sancte Spiritus*, it is said of love, "in labor rest, in mourning comfort." Love is repose that refreshes because the principal office of love is to unite the will of the lover to the beloved. The soul that loves God can suffer trials patiently by saying, "Your will be done." This is the "peace which surpasses all understanding" (Ph 4:7).

In this life everyone must carry his cross, but St. Teresa says that the cross is heavy for him who drags it but not for him who embraces it. Through the help of the Holy Spirit we can endure trials and overcome them.

Thus it is a very good thing to extend our mental prayer throughout the day, as did St. Teresa.

(Affections, prayers and visit to Mary)

VI.

Love is the virtue which gives us strength

"Love is strong as death" (Sg 8:6). As there is no created strength that can resist death, so there is no difficulty for a loving soul that love cannot overcome. When there is a question of pleasing its beloved, love conquers all. Nothing is so hard but that the fire of love can conquer it.

The most certain mark of knowing if a soul really loves God is if it is as faithful in love when things are adverse as when things are prosperous. The saints tell us that God is just as amiable when he chastises as when he consoles us, because he does all for love and for our good. St. John Chrysostom esteemed St. Paul in chains more fortunate than St. Paul rapt up into the third heaven.

Thus the holy martyrs in the midst of their torments rejoiced and thanked God as for the greatest favor that could befall them — suffering for love of him. Other saints proved their love by the penances they performed.

St. Augustine says, "For that which men love, either no labor is felt, or the labor itself is loved."

(Affections, prayers and visit to Mary)

VII.

Love causes God to dwell in our souls

The Holy Spirit is called the "Sweet Guest of the Soul." This was the great promise made by Jesus Christ to those who love him, when he said, "If you love me, you will keep my commandments. And I will ask the Father and he will give you another Advocate to be with you always" (Jn 14:15).

The Holy Spirit never forsakes a soul, says the Council of Trent, if he is not driven away from it: "He does not forsake unless he be first forsaken" (Sess. 5, c. 11).

God, then, dwells in a soul that loves him, but he asks that we love him with our whole hearts. He will have no rivals. As St. James writes, "Or do you suppose that the scripture speaks without meaning when it says, 'The Spirit that he has made to dwell in us tends towards jealousy?'" (Jm 4:5).

Do we wonder if Jesus deserves our whole love? "He gave himself wholly to you," says St. John Chrysostom. "He left nothing for himself." He has given you all his blood and his life; there remains nothing more for him to give you.

(Affections, prayers and visit to Mary)

VIII.

Love is the bond which binds

As the Holy Spirit, who is uncreated love, is the indissoluble bond which binds the Father to the Eternal Word, so he also unites the soul to God. In the words of St. Augustine, "Charity is a virtue uniting us to God." It also means that the love of God unites him to us. How strong is that bond!

The bonds of the world are bonds of death; the bonds of God are bonds of life and salvation. The bonds of God by means of love unite us to God who is our true and only life.

Before the coming of Jesus Christ, men fled from God and turned to earthly goals. But the loving God sent his Son to forge bonds of love. These bonds are the benefits, the lights, the calls to love, the promise of Paradise, but above all, the gift he has bestowed upon us of Jesus Christ in the Sacrifice of the Cross and in the Sacrament of the Altar, and finally, the gift of his Holy Spirit.

"Have charity," says St.Paul, "which is the bond of perfection" (Col 3:14). Love is a bond which unites to itself all other virtues and makes the soul perfect. "Love God and do what you will" is the famous dictum of St. Augustine, because one who loves God tries to avoid causing any displeasure to the beloved and seeks to please him in all things.

(Affections, prayers and visit to Mary)

IX.

Love is a treasure containing every good

Love is that treasure of which the Gospel says that we must leave all things to obtain it, because love make us partakers of the friendship of God: "Those who gain this treasure win the friendship of God" (Ws 7:14). Seek that one good alone which contains in it all other good things. For this we must be detached from worldly goods.

He who finds God finds all that he can desire. "Take delight in the Lord and he will grant you your heart's requests" (Ps 37:4). The human heart is constantly seeking after good things that may make it happy, but if it seeks them from creatures, no matter how much it acquires, it will never be satisfied. If it seeks God alone, God will satisfy all its desires. That is why the saints are the happiest people in the world.

(Affections, prayers and visit to Mary)

X.
The means of loving God and of becoming a saint

The more we love God, the more holy do we become. St. Francis Borgia says that it is prayer that introduces divine love into the human heart. It is mortification that withdraws the heart from the earth and renders it capable of receiving this holy fire of love.

The more there is of earth in the heart the less room there is for holy love. That is why the saints chose mortification to control their self-love and their senses.

But before all, in order to become saints it is necessary to have the desire and the resolution to work at it. The devil may try to make it seem prideful to desire sanctity, and it would be, if we were to rely on our own strength. However, we put our trust in God, saying, "I can do all things in him who strengthens me" (Ph 4:13).

We must, therefore, be of good courage, make strong resolutions, and begin. Prayer can do everything. What we cannot do of our own strength we shall do easily with the help of God, who has promised to give us whatever we ask of him: "If you remain in me and my words remain in you, ask for whatever you want and it will be done for you" (Jn 15:7).

(*Affections, prayers and visit to Mary*)

Prayer to Obtain
the Seven Gifts of the Holy Spirit

Holy Spirit, divine consoler! I adore You as my true God, just as I adore God the Father and God the Son. I unite my praises to those You receive from all the choirs of angels. I offer You my whole heart and I give heartfelt thanks for all the benefits You have given me, and that You continually pour out in the world.

You are the author of all the supernatural gifts, and you have enriched with immense favors the soul of the Blessed Virgin Mary, the Mother of God. I beg You to visit me with Your grace and love.

Grant me the gift of Your *holy fear* in order that it may prevent me from falling any more into my past infidelities for which I now ask You a thousand times to forgive me.

Grant me the gift of *piety* in order that I may in the future serve You with greater fervor, follow with greater promptness Your holy inspirations, and observe with greater exactness Your holy precepts.

Grant me the gift of *knowledge* in order that I may be able to know well the things of God and that, enlightened by Your holy instructions, I may steadily walk in the way of eternal salvation.

Grant me the gift of *fortitude* in order that I may be able courageously to overcome all the attacks of the devil, and escape all the dangers of the world that stand in the way of my eternal salvation.

Grant me the gift of *counsel* in order that I may be able to choose what is most suitable to my spiritual advancement, and to discover all the snares and artifices of the evil spirit who tempts me.

Grant me the gift of *understanding* in order that I may be able to understand better the divine mysteries and, by the contemplation of heavenly things, may detach my thoughts and affections from all the vanities of this world.

Grant me the gift of *wisdom* in order that I may be able to direct all my actions by referring them to God as my last end, so that by loving and serving You in this life as I ought to do, I may have the happiness of eternally possessing You in the next.

Our Father, Hail Mary and the *Glory Be to the Father* three times.

Index